D0377430

Hamish MacInnes has taken part in seven Himalayan expeditions. Three of these were to Mount Everest and during 1975 he was deputy leader of the successful expedition which scaled the South West Face. As well as having been on other expeditions to various parts of the world, including gold prospecting and yeti hunting, he has invented advanced mountain rescue equipment and specialized hardware for high-standard ice climbing.

As leader of the Glencoe Mountain Rescue Team, he plays an active part in rescue work and is the honorary secretary of the Mountain Rescue Committee of Scotland, the founder of the Search and Rescue Dog Association and an honorary member of the Scottish Mountaineering Club. He is one of the authorities on mountain rescue in the world today.

Hamish MacInnes lives in Glencoe and between travelling occupies himself with writing and film planning. In his spare time he develops technical equipment and rescue techniques in the Leishmann Mountain Rescue Research Laboratory, established at his house with the help of the National Trust for Scotland and the government.

Hamish MacInnes

Climb to
the Lost World

Penguin Books

8236

Penguin Books Ltd, Harmondsworth,
Middlesex, England
Penguin Books Australia Ltd, Ringwood,
Victoria, Australia
Penguin Books Canada Ltd,
41 Steelcase Road West, Markham, Ontario, Canada
Penguin Books (N.Z.) Ltd,
182–190 Wairau Road, Auckland 10, New Zealand

First published by Hodder & Stoughton 1974
Published in Penguin Books 1976
Copyright © Hamish MacInnes, 1974

Made and printed in Great Britain by
Hazell Watson & Viney Ltd,
Aylesbury, Bucks
Set in Linotype Georgian

List of Illustrations

Acknowledgements

All other photographs taken by the author

Maps

Author's Note

Without the patience and forbearance of my expedition companions this book would never have been written. Not only had they to endure me in the outback of Guyana, but were on return, pressed at short notice together with John Streetly in checking the MSS which Miss E. Whittome so competently drafted for me.

For years both Adrian Thompson and John Streetly dreamt of a successful expedition to the Prow of Mount Roraima and I share with my friends in their disappointment that John couldn't accompany us. Lastly, without the cooperation and the assistance of the Guyana Government and the services of the Guyana Defence Force our expedition would have collapsed within a stone's throw of our goal.

HM

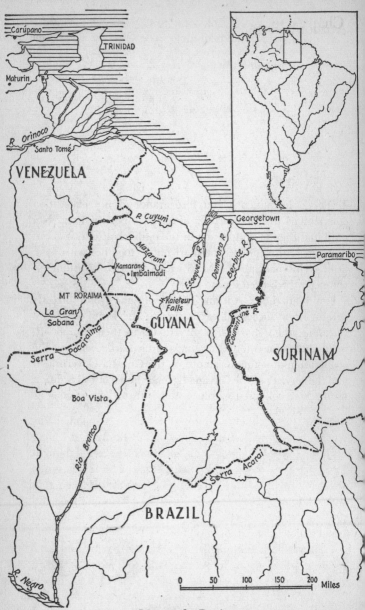

Map of the Region

Chapter 1

I was enformed of the mountain of Christall, to which in trueth for the length of the way, and the evil season of the yeare, I was not able to march, nor abide any longer upon the journey: we saw it farre off and it appeared like a white church towre of an exceeding height.

Sir Walter Raleigh

Spellbound, I watched bromeliads hurtling past me as I clung to the brick-red sandstone face. I was trying to count the number of scorpions which accompanied the flora but swirling mist made this an impossible task. The rock was running with water and the south-east wind which was blowing across the rain forest, 3,000 feet below, was amazingly cold, despite the fact that we were only 5° 15′ north of the Equator.

Six feet above my head, Don Whillans stood like a statue on a ledge barely the width of his boot; his solid figure, clothed in an orange waterproof suit, gave to the place a comforting sense of reality. From above in the ghastly Bottomless Chimney came the distorted shouts of Joe Brown and Mo Anthoine. I knew they were having a desperate time, but we could do nothing to help. I was still badly shaken by ten of the worst minutes of my life, and as I hung on a microscopic ledge, I wondered what the hell I thought I was doing up there on the Great Prow of Mount Roraima – Conan Doyle's 'Lost World'. The partially severed rope with water streaming down it, up which I'd just climbed, did nothing to reassure me. Obviously, it seemed, my first instinct had been the right one.

That was back at home in Glencoe in October 1969 when I received a letter from John Streetly, an old climbing friend with whom I'd been on the North Face of the Grande

Jorasses. John lives in Trinidad and I opened his letter with pleasurable anticipation. John never writes unless prompted by some exciting enterprise. 'Dear Hamish,' it ran

I feel that we have just the thing for you down here. You may recall that, about three years ago, I went into the rain forest area on the Brazil/Guyana border to climb a 'Lost World' type of overhanging mesa which offered an atmosphere very similar to that in Conan Doyle's story and involved us in some rather spectacular overhanging rock climbing. These mountains (5,000–10,000 feet) overhang all round the perimeter and, in some places, the water from the top of the plateau falls nearly 1,500 feet to the bottom of the cliffs. The scenery and the wild life is phenomenal.

There are still at least two unclimbed peaks in the Roraima area and I enclose some photographs to give you an idea of the terrain. I have some good contacts in Guyana and, if you're interested, we could get something arranged during the dry season. Adrian Thompson, from the Guyana Government Service, wants to organize a trip to the south face of Roraima next spring. What chance of you joining us? Write soon ...

But at that time I was too full of plans to go to the Russian Caucasus to be able to work up enthusiasm for the sandstone towers with overhanging jungle tops depicted in John's photographs. And anyway I'd heard terrifying tales of the wild life, and visualized John's mesas seething with deadly snakes.

Early in 1973 I had a visit from Julian Anthoine, who everyone calls Mo. He was bringing me a glass fibre capsule which he had produced as a possible design for a new type of stretcher to evacuate injured climbers from high cliffs. Mo, who is thirty-three, is small and dark with an almost uncontrollable exuberance which has carried him all over the world. He is always getting in and out of scrapes and has, to say the least, a picturesque way of putting things and a bawdy sense of humour.

Mo told me that he was going to Roraima in Guyana, to tackle the Great Prow. Roraima's summit marks Guyana's border with Venezuela and Brazil. The Prow is an over-hanging buttress of sandstone which would perhaps give the only possible access from Guyana to the country's section of the summit. Adrian Thompson and Don Whillans were to be joint leaders of the party which was also to include John Streetly, Joe Brown and Mike Thompson, who had been on the Annapurna South Face expedition. It was obviously going to be a strong team. I offered Mo my condolences, however, for I still had a vivid picture of scorpions and spiders printed indelibly on my mind.

'One thing, Mo,' I said with conviction. 'You wouldn't get me there!'

At the time I hoped to go back to the south-west face of Everest with the Japanese expedition in the fall of 1973 and I wondered as I spoke to Mo which would be the most gruelling trip: the inhospitable wastes of that great unclimbed face of Everest with its rarified air and atrocious weather of the post-monsoon period, or the incessant rain and blood-curdling creepy-crawlies of the Roraima region.

Mo returned south to his climbing equipment business in Llanberis and a cold spring followed, during which I was working on a film on Buachaille Etive Mor in Glencoe for a television drama series called *Sutherland's Law* with Ian Cuthbertson playing the leading role in a climbing murder story. Neil McCallum was the producer and had many years previously made *Hazard*, a climbing film set in the Dolomites, with Joe Brown.

Then I heard that the Japanese Alpine Club had decided not to invite Dougal Haston and me on their Everest expedition since recent history of joint expeditions had been, to put it mildly, disastrous. They were very apologetic about it and felt sure we would understand. We did! Dougal had been a member of the ill-fated International expedition of 1971 and I had been on the German expedition in 1973 with Don Whillans and Doug Scott. Both Dougal and I had climbed together on Chris Bonnington's expedition during the post-monsoon expedition in 1973 and were still keen to have another crack at that terrible, but fascinating face. It was not to be.

My old friend Don Whillans came up to Glencoe at the end of May, on his annual pilgrimage to the 'tribes of the north', as he calls us. This time he'd brought a caravan, an appendage of modern motoring for which I, in common with many Highland Scots, have an inborn hatred. Don, even after knowing me for many years, still believes I live on potatoes and porridge; on the other hand, I have to admit that I too am prejudiced, for I assume that he lives solely on beer and fags. He stopped outside my house, leaving his caravan parked by the side of the main road.

'Ah thocht ye were oot, Jock,' he said as he came in, then rapidly abandoned the unaccustomed dialect, 'How goes it?'

'Not bad, old fruit,' I replied. 'I see you have a mobile home these days – just in time to join the caravan Lemming Meet at Mallaig; they're all going to drive off the pier.'

'Your jokes are worse than ever,' he spat out. 'Where can I park the bloody thing?'

Kingshouse Hotel is always a congenial meeting place in Glencoe; particularly so during this period, since the BBC actors and crew had virtually taken over the whole hotel. Mo had met Neil McCallum there once, but on that occasion we hadn't had an opportunity to discuss the expedition. Now Don came up with me one evening and met Neil, a Canadian by birth but a Scotsman by ancestry and inclination. Don, in his dry way, told us of his forthcoming trip to Conan Doyle's 'Lost World'.

'Aye, we've got quite a bit of backing from the Government out there,' he drawled in his broad Mancunian accent as he put down his pint of Tartan with deliberation. 'It makes me suspicious. I think there's a fair chance that the Venezuelans may send in a reception committee to welcome us with blow pipes.'

'Why?' I asked, my interest instantly roused. 'Is there political trouble out there?'

'Oh, aye,' said Don. 'I think there are a few fly moves afoot. There's always been trouble with that ruddy mountain. You see, the Guyana bods can't get to the top except through Venezuela and the Venezuelans aren't that friendly.'

I remembered John Streetly telling me of a place where the top of a peak was covered in agates and so I asked Don if there was any chance of diamonds.

'Tons of them,' he replied. 'It's the second biggest diamond area of the world!'

I could see Neil's interest was being roused and the diamonds certainly intrigued me – a throwback, no doubt, to a lot of futile prospecting I once did in New Zealand.

I hadn't admitted it to anyone, but ever since Mo was staying with me in the winter, the Roraima expedition had been getting under my skin. Out of sheer perversity I had made a point of saying to several friends, 'What a place to go! Goodness, it's wet enough in Scotland but at least when it's wet here we don't get midges and tourists. There you get everything all the time.'

However, I hadn't succeeded in fooling myself, as I quickly realized, listening to Don speaking in a monotone which, in any other person would have been extremely dull; but Don's speech becomes compulsive listening, and makes him probably one of the most popular lecturers in the climbing world today.

'Aye, we haven't all that much brass,' I heard him say to Neil. 'It's an expensive trip and we haven't got round to doing much about raising any of the necessary.'

It was at this point in proceedings I found myself suggesting to Neil that we make a film of the trip. With our contacts in the BBC we could surely swing something.

Neil is one of the most charitable men I have ever met; he

said that he would do his best to try and arrange a meeting with Bob Coulter, Controller, BBC Scotland, and would contact the former Controller, Alasdair Milne, who has now moved to London in charge of BBC2. Both would be powerful allies.

Neil has had a hard life; brought up in the wilds of Saskatchewan, he has starred in several popular television series and his role in the *Mad Trapper*, a drama set in the wild North West Territories, won him wide acclaim. Some of his other ploys have not been so successful. A notable failure was his Spanish pram scheme. Whilst on a visit to Spain he observed that many holiday makers had difficulty in transporting their offspring to the desired beach location for the day's sunbathing and swimming. Neil felt certain that a scheme involving a massive import of folding prams, with plastic tracks which fitted over the two pairs of wheels should enable perambulation over the most awkward terrain by frustrated parents, and incidentally would make him a fortune. Loads of prams and plastic tracks were dispatched to Spanish warehouses whilst Neil drew up his plans. But the project was finally thwarted by the Spanish Government who refused Neil permission to operate in Spain; however they saw fit to start the venture themselves!

Almost without realizing it, I had become deeply involved in the Lost World expedition. My acceptance of the fact was probably mainly due to Don and Joe Brown; I had known them both a long time and we all got on well together. There is always a lack of solemnity in their company and an invigorating casualness which is most enjoyable. Joe Brown has been called the human fly. He is a rock specialist, not caring overmuch for snow and ice climbing. That's his story, but it should be remembered that he succeeded in climbing Kangchenjunga, the third highest mountain in the world, and the Mustagh Tower in the Karakorams, to say nothing of Mount Communism in the Pamirs.

Joe at forty-three is an easy-going individual; never wanting to hurt people's feelings, yet never shirking a difficult decision, always ready to laugh or take part in any riotous fun or practical joke; great company. He becomes totally absorbed in his hobby, whether it be canoeing, fishing, or climbing and in a very short time he becomes master of the sport. Fundamentally, he is highly competitive and will try his damnedest to beat one in any frivolous competition. He has a razor-sharp and inquiring brain, will never accept facts at face value and is capable of rapid and accurate mental calculations. He now owns two sports shops in North Wales which his wife Val manages; this leaves him more time to pursue his hobbies and work on building and extending his property. Like me, he needs to work with his hands rather than be bogged down with paper work. But, for Joe the hard years are past.

Don is in many ways the complete opposite. Blunt and shrewd, tending to introversion, he is at the same time gregarious: at his best in a desperate mountain crisis or holding forth in a pub where he can talk and drink at great length. I have always maintained that Don, in his day, was one of the greatest mountaineers. Frequently, he remains in the background, almost free-wheeling, until the odds are against him when he comes forth with unbelievable reserves of will-power and endurance. It was an education to climb with him on Everest. He was grossly overweight even when he arrived at Base Camp, having previously stated in a television interview when asked when he stopped drinking, 'At the last pub – Namche Bazaar'.

He took his time, acclimatizing slowly and summing up the situation, which he always does with great perception. It is when others are starting to feel the colossal strain of high altitude climbing that he comes into his own. He is pared down to his proper weight, having lost about two stones in five weeks, and starts going like a bomb. Don has unfortunately a very bad reputation, most of which is ill-founded. During the farcical 1971 International Everest expedition he was labelled the 'evil genius of Everest' but there are always two sides to any argument: when Don eventually writes about that ill-fated trip it will be shown that the more temperamental French were largely to blame for the downfall of the expedition. Don is an amazingly straight bloke. There can be no pretence with him, he sees right through any hypocrisy: that is the time to beware for he won't beat about the bush, no matter who is involved. I have been in many dangerous situations with him – and no doubt will be in the future – but I cannot think of anyone better with whom to share a tight corner.

Don, now forty, had many false attempts at conventional jobs which didn't suit his temperament (both Joe and Don were plumbers in the past); eventually he has found a niche which seems to suit him, as a director of a clothing business which specializes in golfing and climbing weather wear. This allows him enough time off to indulge in expeditions for, as he remarked, 'Aye, lad, if you don't get away on a trip at least once a year, you get stale.' While at home, he tours the country as a highly successful and very dead-pan lecturer.

Neil and I worried at the Lost World project whenever we had a chance between filming and became more and more enthusiastic. The BBC agreed to put up some money and to send Neil as director in charge of a two-man film crew. I myself could, if necessary, film the climb to the summit. We were getting cooperative noises from the GPO about the possibility of first day covers and were even contemplating making up our funds by auctioning the diamonds we would be bringing back from the summit at Christie's. 'I've seen a lot of bright buggers with bright ideas in my life,' was Don's dry reaction, as we reported to him at Troon when he came up to promote his golf wear at the Open.

About this time the members of the proposed Roraima expedition were scattered widely over the face of the earth. Mo had already gone to the Alps; Joe was going to France on a holiday and Don was going on a cruise to the Greek islands. Mike Thompson was going to the Central Himalayas on a recce for a possible new Cook's Tour which was to commence in 1974. Neil was going to Italy for a well-earned rest, while I was due to go and do some work for the BBC with Dougal Haston on the north face of the Eiger. One can hardly call it chaos when there was nobody there to observe the mess, but certainly, over the next few weeks, the expedition was only supported by the rising mountain of mail, bills and 'urgent' queries from Guyana and all over this country. We had no food supplies since we had heard that most foodstuffs were prohibited entry to Guyana, and the equipment was hurriedly transported by Mo in a small van, reaching the Liverpool docks just in time to catch a freighter bound for Georgetown.

Adrian Thompson contacted Mike just before he left for India, explaining that permission had been obtained from the Government to import all expedition foodstuffs free of duty. An enormous panic ensued. Mike couldn't possibly buy and pack the food in the remaining few hours before the ship's departure, so he contacted the shipping company who went to the supermarkets and managed to buy £300-worth of food in a couple of hours. We are greatly indebted to them for this remarkable feat.

The newspaper and magazine rights had already been sold to the *Observer*; this would present few problems since both Don and I had worked before with Jeremy Hunt, of the *Observer* staff. Our Everest reports had been sent to him. There was a suggestion from Jeremy that Chris Brasher should come out with us as reporter to the expedition. However, we didn't see a great deal of point in this, as Chris wouldn't have managed to get up the Wall; we were going to be extremely lucky if we could get up the face ourselves. We were, as our friends had been at pains to point out, most of us a bit long in the tooth.

Meanwhile Neil, always the comedian, was going about

the BBC slapping himself and pulling out imaginary poisoned darts, and I in my ever practical way had been trying to get us nylon boiler suits to keep the beasties at bay on the cliff face. Don was very scathing about these and, considering the temperature when we'd be wearing them, rechristened them boiling suits immediately.

Earlier I had suggested to Adrian that a helicopter should be chartered to take all the filming and climbing equipment to base camp, as this would be cheaper and simpler than hiring Indians. I now heard that he'd fixed this and won a great deal of support from the Guyana Government, including flights into the interior and free water travel by canoe. Adrian had telephoned me at 2.30 a.m. to give me these glad tidings. They had officially approved our expedition at a Cabinet meeting that day. This cleared the way for a speedy departure to our objective, once we arrived in Georgetown, while for our arrival Adrian had a senior custom officer lined up to deal specifically with our gear. It really looked as if we were to get the red carpet treatment. Typically, it was only Don who paused to wonder why.

Chapter 2

But follow; let the torrent dance thee down
To find him in the valley; let the wild
Lean-headed eagles yelp alone, and leave
The monstrous ledges there to slope and spill
Their thousand wreaths of dangling water smoke,
That like a broken purpose waste in air:

'The Princess', *Tennyson*

When I returned home from the Eiger it was to find that the BBC had been obliged to cut their financial contribution to the expedition by one third due to spiralling production costs. This was a severe blow, but the Film Department at BBC Glasgow made an amazingly good choice of film crew when they finally decided to send Alex Scott and Gordon Forsyth. Not only did the two men get on well with everyone on the expedition but they were also technicians of the highest calibre. Their dedication to their work – the film – was almost unbelievable; even when half-starving and depressed by the jungle terrain, with that continuous oppressive sense of being hemmed in by the bush; the job always came first.

Alex is a thin aesthetic figure, almost delicate in appearance which belies his stamina and endurance; though after experiencing some hard trips one learns to recognize it more often in the lean man than in the athletic and muscular. He possesses the resilience of young bamboo and a keen mind always ready to grapple with a problem. Gordon and he had mutual interests in hi-fi and photography; they would converse together for hours on these topics. I had worked with Alex before and knew him to be one of the most able cameramen in the country. Gordon is as robust as Alex is weak-looking. He gives the impression of just having emerged from a bath, scrubbed clean and shining, his clothes always immaculate (even in the worst swamps of the march). Sturdily built, with a shock of wavy hair, his practice of yoga is reflected in his healthy appearance. Both men are meticulous in their toilets, compared to climbers who may have to forgo a wash for long periods on high mountains and frequently revel in the fact.

Gordon had just returned, three weeks previously, from filming on an expedition to Greenland with the Simpsons, an adventurous family who enjoy roughing it in Arctic wastes. He had carried his Nagra tape recorder, an awkward twenty-lb. load, on his back throughout the trip, except when they were canoeing, and was therefore in fine shape for our expedition.

There were lengthy discussions at the BBC as to which cameras should be taken. Finally it was decided to take an Ariflex BL, an Eclair, a Bell and Howell 70DR, and two twin lens autoloads, small magazine loading cameras, for use on the face and summit. On the whole, a good choice though, when it came to it, the large BL was never used on the mountain. Gordon was pinning his tape recording faith to his trusty Nagra but he also had the miniature Nagra SN, a minute high quality recorder: one which I had used on Everest in temperatures of $-35°C$. Being a perfectionist, Gordon was reluctant to use it, although the quality would have satisfied most men. As it happens, water was to be the problem on Roraima, not frost. We took various still cameras besides, which were chosen on a personal basis. Joe, Don and Mo decided to take underwater cameras (Neil thought that they were being unduly pessimistic!). Gordon took a BBC Nikon and I gave a loan of the *Observer*'s Canon to Alex for black and white photography whilst I used a Rollex SLR with several of the new multi-coated lenses.

Don had assumed the role of doctor ('God help us,' I thought) and sent me anti-malarial tablets; I passed some on to the BBC contingent. However, due to the fact that I was so busy prior to departure, I neglected to take any myself. I

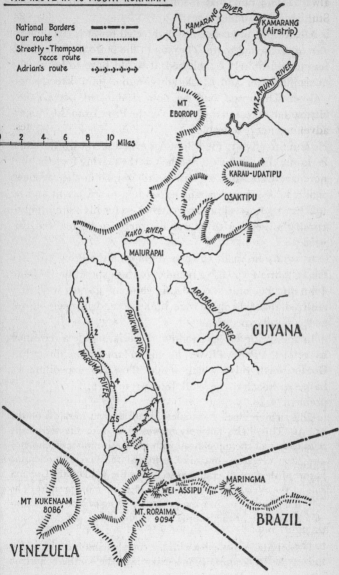

THE ROUTE IN TO MOUNT RORAIMA

National Borders
Our route
Streetly-Thompson
recce route
Adrian's route

0 2 4 6 8 10 Miles

KAMARANG RIVER

KAMARANG
(Airstrip)

MAZARUNI RIVER

MT
EBOROPU

KARAU-UDATIPU

OSAKTIPU

KAKO RIVER

MAIURAPAI

PAIKWA RIVER

ARABARU RIVER

GUYANA

△1

△2

△3

MARUMA RIVER

△4

△5

6

7
8

WEI-ASSIPU

MARINGMA

MT KUKENAAM
8086'

MT RORAIMA
9094'

BRAZIL

VENEZUELA

tried to find out what medical supplies we did have, but without any notable success.

Meanwhile, my concern was directed towards the difficulties of the actual route. The way to the bottom of the climb was now definitely established. It would have to be via the Waruma River and El Dorado Swamp. John Streetly and Adrian Thompson had by now established beyond any doubt that access to the bottom of the Prow from the Paikwa River was not practicable.

John Streetly's name will be for ever linked with Roraima, certainly the north side, and he was the driving force behind our expedition. But we now heard from him the sad news that a knee injury was not responding to treatment and he was having to go about on crutches, so his life's ambition to climb the Prow with us was not going to be realized this year.

In 1972 John made the first attempt on the Prow with Bev Clark. Adrian was also a member of this expedition. Though John and Bev only succeeded in climbing a short way, they realized the difficulties were immense and insuperable for such a small expedition.

In the spring of 1973 John and Adrian made a reconnaisance of the Paikwa River, hoping to find a more direct line to the north ridge which would allow our expedition an easier approach to the Wall. John wrote later:

This time we made a complete circuit around Roraima on the way in. This flight, not only impressed us with the terrifically wild terrain of the top plateau with its massive water catchments and deep crevasses, but also restressed the fierce, unrelenting nature of the face. Overall that section of the Wall on the Guyana side of the Weiassipu col seemed to offer the most promise. The return flight took us over the Savannahs lying east of the Paikwa which we thought might provide a landing ground for light aircraft ...

We left Maiurapai early with the complex and intriguing skyline of the Pakaraimas silhouetted across the southern horizon ahead. We crossed from savannah into scrub and then into forest proper, eventually coming across a trail and within three hours were through to the Paikwa ... Without having attempted it, no one can appreciate the difficulties in trying to hold a compass course in heavily wooded rain forest bisected by steep, muddy creeks and overrun with short bamboo. We had lost more than three hours in this area before relocating the trail, but were rewarded however by finding a most beautiful riverside campsite that evening. Alfred, our guide, told us that this was the furthest point of Amerindian habitation along the Paikwa. No one to his knowledge had travelled far beyond this point, which was called Kaplagung, after the name of the old Indian who, legend had it, used to live there. The river gravel here was delicately coloured, containing boulders of green and red jasper and the exposures of normal Roraima sandstone were less apparent.

We were now in completely unexplored country as we continued along the river, cutting our way through areas of fine tight bamboo. After about three hours of this, Alfred in the lead leapt away to one side crashing through the bush and yelling at us to stay away from a nasty-looking coiled snake which Adrian quickly blew apart with his shotgun. The snake turned out to be a labarria (fer de lance), its fangs over an inch long. This incident upset the Indians very much as the only thing they seemed to fear in the jungle is a labarria or a bushmaster. A bite from either of these snakes is almost invariably fatal.

Farther up-river the going became heavier. We had been unable to get a fix for the past two days and were uncertain as to the point at which we should turn right up to the main tributary of the Paikwa. The going continued to get heavier and dirtier with a great deal of steep ground to cover. Eventually from a spur of the ridge we managed to get a restricted view of Weiassipu which indicated that we were, as we expected, east of the col and not in a good position to rectify this error.

After a long hard day, camp was eventually set just above a very pleasant side stream with clear, running water cutting through the rock and cascading down into the Paikwa river about 600 feet below. As we came on to the edge of the first waterfall, one of the Indians called Renton shouted, 'Look at Roraima!' The shout flushed two powis which, apparently being completely unused to man, merely flew up to the trees and were quickly potted for dinner. The sight of Roraima confirmed our position but the cloud drifted over again preventing a good view of the climbing possibilities.

Adrian and I wandered down for a wash in the stream and examined the formation through which it had cut its course – a series of big flat steps cascading down to the Paikwa gorge. Just upstream of the camp was a very beautiful pool of clear water contained in a worn out hollow of pure green jasper, the sides and bottom glowing translucent green in the evening light. To complete the picture there were masses of flowers of all colours around the edge of the pool cascading down almost into the water. Downstream across the valley the main tributary of the Paikwa crashed down a massive fall into the gorge from the Roraima cliffs. Below us the Paikwa itself roared through a gully about a hundred feet deep and sixty feet wide, cut through the jasper formation, and the evening sun highlighted the green glow coming up from the chasm.

Friday morning was dull and cloudy, but we still needed to have a good look at the Roraima wall so we left Jasper Creek camp at dawn. The going was very wet and heavy with still no sight of the mountain. The terrain kept forcing us up to the left to keep out of the steep gorges of the river. We had to do a lot of cutting and we had to haul ourselves up the rocks from root to root.

After about two hours the sound of a shot rang out and a flashing orange bird crashed to the ground just ahead of us. Renton ran forward and picked up a cock-of-the-rock, one of the most beautiful birds of the South American jungle. These birds are protected but in Amerindian reservations they are eagerly sought for use in the decoration of ceremonial head-dresses and, pity though it is, it is not illegal for the Amerindians to shoot them.

We were gaining height fast now but still without sight of Roraima. Eventually about noon we were able to clear the trees from a subsidiary spur and see that we were approximately on a level with the Wei-Assipu col and just below the ridge which marked the Brazilian border.

The cloud remained thick around us and although we waited

for some time it showed no indication of lifting. As we had travelled light we were not in a position to set up another camp, but we had established the fact that this was a feasible route to the Wei-Assipu col and that under the circumstances our second attempt on Roraima would have to follow the original route.

Though the lower Paikwa trail was comparatively good, the upper section of the watershed did not afford feasible access to the northern cliffs of Roraima, and both John and Adrian realized that the original trail, which had been pioneered by Bailey of the Geological Survey, was the only route to our objective.

John's return route still had some surprises in store which should be a warning for us:

Within five minutes of Jasper Creek camp, with Adrian just ahead of me, I lurched heavily against a sapling and put my right hand to steady myself. Looking down to watch placement of my foot, I saw a coiled bushmaster, head raised to thigh level ready to strike at my right leg as it swung past the sapling. Lethargy disappeared in a flash and swinging to the left, I knocked Renton flying, avoiding what must have been an almost definite fatality from the seven-foot snake. Our yells brought Phillip rushing back with a gun and I was able to blow off the head of the snake just below the neck and examine the one and a half inch fangs with venom already dripping out of the ends. It was ironic that this danger should exist so close to what must have been one of the most beautiful places on the face of the earth.

But as well as excitements, they also had some interesting conversations with the Indians in the evenings at the end of the day's march:

Alfred talked about the morning star Ka-ha-nuk and the 'five little stars' (his stories reminiscent of those told about the ancient Polynesian navigators). The 'five little stars' when low in the sky indicated the season for certain birds and the position of Ka-ha-nuk also indicated the advent of the rains. We were shown the labba lights, a fungus growing on roots and on the forest floor, which glowed brightly in the dark. We learned to identify the incense-like resin which the Indians used for lighting fires. The bright orange, smoky scented flame was also used as a night light. Alfred and Renton showed us leaves which were used to heal cuts – in this way our education progressed!

But writing to us at the time, John dismissed the Paikwa Reconnaisance by saying that it was no go and lots of snakes. Don had passed on to me several photographs of the Prow, and whenever I had a moment I studied them for possible lines up the face; it seemed to bristle with overhangs, and I felt sure the climb would take at least three weeks. In the event every fear was justified. We were faced by highly technical climbing.

Joe reassured me that we were taking plenty of bolts and some hand drills and I arranged for us to get two Hilti guns. These fire a piston that can only travel an inch or so and this drives the bolt home without the danger of killing anyone else in the immediate vicinity.

Two representatives from the Hilti Company duly appeared in Glencoe. With the aid of a local geologist, we tried out the guns, firing bolts into cracks in hard limestone which we assumed mistakenly, to be similar in hardness to the sandstone of Roraima. The tools worked perfectly and we tested the bolts to loads of over 1,500 lb. The firm was only too pleased to let us have two guns on loan for the duration of the trip, plus a thousand cartridges and bolts. Several days later two red steel containers, like attaché cases, arrived, each weighing about 60 lb.: the bolt guns. Feeling their weight with alarm, I hastily decided they must be taken as 'inconspicuous' hand luggage on the flight!

Admitting that his diamond auction scheme might not be entirely practicable, Neil set his agile brain to work again on money-making possibilities for the trip. His schemes were numerous, but a fortnight was scarcely an adequate period in which to implement them. He had been in touch with the GPO before he went on holiday to discuss the possibility of first day covers. He contacted them again when he returned and found that they had prepared for this last minute eventuality, and had optimistically been in touch with the Guyana postal authorities. But somehow (I never really found out why), the official wires got crossed and the outcome was that the Guyana GPO, in a fit of pique, decided to issue their own first day cover. They planned to set up a 'Post Office' on the summit of Roraima (by helicopter) so that the first day covers would be stamped on the very day that we climbers appeared dripping over the scorpion-infested edge. Adrian was to be given a crash course on franking and sworn in as an honorary postmaster. Obviously the Guyanan GPO were no sluggards when it came to economizing! Neil's idea was nationalized before we even left Britain! 'Just like your pram idea Neil,' I said.

So we were now left with 3,000 superb envelopes which bore the title 'BBC Roraima Expedition to the Lost World, 1973' and were liberally endowed with waterfalls, pterodactyls, and exotic palms. Neil had persuaded one of his script writers to compose the following insert:

RORAIMA : *The last great adventure left*

The Legend
There was always the legend. In a continent of legends; like Eldorado, the gilded, where the supposed king of Manoa was covered with oil and powdered with gold dust so that he became literally a figure of gold in a city where the precious metal was as common as the dust on the ground; like the legends of the Inca and their fabled empire which the Conquistadors proved to be fact; there was the legend of Roraima, Mother of the Great Waters, a fabled mountain plateau in the depths of the jungle north of the Matto Grosso, west of Guyana, perhaps near to the fabled Eldorado itself. Roraima guarded by jungle and swamp, by a sea of green, the great rain forests of the interior, is believed to be the source of all diamonds in the area but fear of evil spirits prevented the Indians venturing near it. The legend was further

added to by Conan Doyle in 1912 when he wrote *The Lost World*, envisaging the plateau as being the haunt of monsters of prehistory, unchanged since the palaeozoic period. Since the dawn of time itself, there was the legend. And since the dawn of time man has strived to find and climb the great mountain.

The Reality

Roraima exists. Deep in the interior of Guyana at the conjunction of that country with Venezuela and Brazil it rises more than 9,000 feet above sea level, a plateau twenty-five miles square created by the vast changing forces of nature some 1,750 million years ago. It is indeed the Mother of Waters with its cascading falls creating the rivers of the forests. Its forbidding, eroded rock summit isolated by sheer towering rock faces, its base is surrounded by mud swamps merging into the great rain forests teeming with snakes, scorpions and poisonous spiders ...

Despite the postal defeat, Neil was ecstatic during this period, still removing imaginary darts. I was frequently with him in his office at Broadcasting House where messages flew out right, left, and centre, via Dorothy, his secretary, while a worn-out record of Mozart's Flute Concerto – one of Neil's favourites – blared out from the record player on the floor.

'Where are the boiler suits?' someone would shout.

'What size of longjohns does Gordon need?'

'I've a good line in mosy-nets,' I offered. 'They hang over your hat – ten pence each.'

'Yes, the BBC medical officer will arrange for the vaccinations for Cholera and Yellow Fever for the BBC team – tomorrow at 2 p.m. – Yes.'

One evening I did a short news programme for BBC Television which resulted in a host of letters arriving during the next few days. One of these shook me somewhat. It was from a Dr McInnes Fletcher who, incidentally, had named his house in Inverness 'Roraima'. He was eloquent about snakes:

Snakes. While there are many snakes of all types and sizes the most dangerous is without doubt the Bushmaster which is a black snake about eight to ten feet long, has very long teeth or fangs which can even penetrate a leather shoe, the poison is deadly in two to five minutes, and it is also one of the very few snakes that attack you. This is because it has a nest and guards its young. You can reckon on meeting one within fifty yards of entering a pathway into the forest as it acts as sentinel! I personally stopped its attack by simply swinging a walking stick slowly from side to side. Very effective and no need to kill the poor thing. Also there is the rattlesnake which is normally referred to as the grass snake, so use a walking stick to thump the ground as vibration is more important to a snake, so it runs away. As for the water Camoudi it has no poison, but nevertheless can crush its victim to death by entwining itself around the body. I've seen samples up to twenty-six feet, and some are reputed to grow to thirty or forty feet. I have seen one crush a Jaguar to death. So carry a knife to cut it in pieces should anyone get snared. It is for the most part about streams and rivers and creeks. Then beware of the Kaboura fly which is even smaller than the West Highland midge, and infinitely more vicious. Your skin rises in multiple pimples which take about six weeks to subside. Only found in the vicinity of water which is a relief.

And lastly but by no means least of all your team should be vaccinated against Paralytic Rabies which is transmitted by the evil Vampire Bat which bloodsucks both cattle and humans at dusk and early morning without either feeling that it is happening ... While in the interior it is often preferable to sleep in hammocks, slung between two trees, and with a 'collar' on each end of the rope so as to prevent snakes crawling in. The hammock has the additional advantage of keeping the *Ants* at bay as they seem to be present everywhere in tropical America.

I trust you will find the above information useful, and should you be interested in any other aspect please contact me. Above all, please try and avoid the rainy season, as out there it is regarded as being fit only for mad dogs and Englishmen.

He also sent me a booklet which he had published, *Some Diseases and Problems of Veterinary Interest in Tropical America*, which lent confirmation to my misgivings:

Rabies in Central and South America takes the form of what is known as Paralytic Rabies, a form which is transmitted to cattle by the evil Vampire Bat which lives and multiplies by bloodsucking herbivorous animals for the most part, and so passes on the disease via its saliva which is infective for virus when the bat itself is infected. There are three species of Vampire Bats, usually referred to as Haemotophagus Bats, these being – Desmodus rotundus, known as the common vampire bat; Diphylla ecuadata, the hairy legged vampire bat; and Diomus youngeii, the white spotted vampire bat which is partial to the Avian species of animals and so is not so important from a disease angle as the other two.

There have been many recorded cases of Rabies in human beings in Central and South America.

The booklet lists three points under the comforting heading 'Preventative Measures in Humans', but adds this warning to the entry under General Treatment: 'This treatment is rather severe on the general system and may give rise to a general reaction with occasionally post-vaccination paralysis from which the patient may or may not recover. It is therefore preferable that all personnel handling Rabies in any way should be protected beforehand with a safe and reliable vaccine for human beings. The writer was protected with the 200 th. Duck Egg passaged Flury Strain modified live virus vaccine.'

My first reaction was to telephone our local doctor:

'Dr MacKenzie, have you any idea where I can get a vaccine for Paralytic Rabies?'

'For what?' he replied, considerably startled although by now fairly accustomed to my outlandish requests.

'Paralytic Rabies,' I reiterated patiently. 'I'm off to South America and this vaccine has been recommended to me; apparently there are vampire bats in the region that we're visiting.'

'I must say, you have some strange ideas of a holiday,

Hamish! I can only suggest that you contact the Medical Officer of Health in Oban; he may be able to suggest something. By the way, your TAB vaccine has arrived; you can come down whenever it's convenient for you.'

'Many thanks,' I answered gratefully.

I was eventually put on to a senior doctor of the Home and Health Department in Edinburgh. No doubt he had read of some of my rather mad exploits in the past, as he voiced little surprise at my request, although he doubted if such a vaccine was readily available. He promised to ring me back ... True to his word, he telephoned later that day and told me he had procured the necessary vaccine; he had arranged an appointment for us to be vaccinated at the Corporation of Glasgow Health Department the following day. Gordon, Alex and I went to Glasgow but Neil, who had to return south, hoped to get his done in London instead. (This later proved impossible to arrange). As for the rest of the expedition members, they weren't able to fix it up in the time. Don and Mike were still abroad while Mo and Joe were in Llanberis in North Wales, with no opportunity of having the vaccine.

From books, I gleaned more information on these blood sucking fiends. It is said (presumably by those who told their story before dying!) that the vampire has a soporific effect on its victim but that the infected bats have a painful bite, whereas a normal Desmodus's attentions are completely painless and it takes its meal with the minimum discomfort to the unwary donor. These bats are also known to carry Chagas's disease, the horrible malady from which Darwin died. In some areas, apparently, bats have been artificially infected with Yellow Fever, which did not help to endear them to me either.

It caused a considerable stir in the Health Centre when we three intrepid explorers marched in for our vaccination, trying to look unconcerned. We were told to sit down and relax, after being ceremoniously ushered past a long queue. Then each of us in turn was taken into a room and, somewhat surprised, was asked to lie down on a couch and bare the tummy while 1 cc. of Duck Embryo Vaccine was injected. This was obviously a novel task for the doctor and the nurses treated us cautiously as if, at any minute, we might start hanging upside down from the curtain rails!

And when it was all over and we were all feeling equal parts sore and apprehensive the doctor blandly informed us that the dose wouldn't be effective for six weeks and we should get ourselves another one in six months' time. 'Wait till Don hears about this,' I thought ruefully. 'He'll piss himself laughing!'

I had just gone home to Glencoe that night when Don rang and our medical misfortunes were forgotten in another crisis. Mike Thompson was supposed to have organized the tickets, but he was still in India and only proposed being back in Britain for less than a day before going out ahead of us with Mo to try and sort out the food and gear.

So another crisis followed and was eventually solved and each day took us nearer our deadline for departure, with everything still in a state of panic. Nevertheless, I have always maintained that the most interesting trips are those which are not overorganized – ours certainly wasn't! At least, disorganization guarantees a certain number of problems which add spice to a hare-brained enterprise.

Chris Brasher had decided definitely not to come on the expedition, as reporting from the base of the Wall only would have little impact. So Jeremy Hunt of the *Observer* suggested that I should send back weekly reports with photographs, using a series of Amerindian runners and a military plane to get them back to Georgetown.

Our trip was getting more like Conan Doyle's Lost World expedition every day, and I was obviously being cast as Ed Malone of the *Daily Gazette*. 'That stalwart newshound of the cleft sticks,' as Neil put it. We wondered if Adrian

Thompson, whom we had not yet met, would fit the part of that deadly shot, Lord Roxton of the Savage Club.

'And how about Don for Professor Challenger?'

Chapter 3   We were within seven miles from an enormous
line of ruddy cliffs which encircled, beyond all
doubt, the plateau of which Professor Challenger
spoke.

'The Lost World', *Sir Arthur Conan Doyle*

Of course Conan Doyle wasn't the first Englishman to be
inspired by the Roraima legends. Nor was he the first to
moot the lost world theory. In 1884 Sir Joseph Hooker suggested that the flora of the Roraima plateau would differ
considerably from that of the plain and newspaper cor-
respondents took this a stage further, hinting that prehistoric
monsters might even make their home on Roraima's summit, having been suspended in their evolutionary develop-
ment. Back in 1874 the *Spectator* had noted:

Will no one explore Roraima and bring back to us the tidings
which it has been waiting these thousands of years to give us?
One of the great marvels of the mysteries of the Earth lies on
the outskirts of one of our colonies – British Guiana – and we
leave the mystery unsolved, the marvel uncared for.

A stirring plea, but easier made than answered.

Sir Walter Raleigh was probably the first white man to
write about the area, although it is doubtful if he ever actually saw the mountain. He wrote, as follows:

I was enformed of the mountain of Christall, to which in
trueth for the length of the way, and the evil season of the yeare,
I was not able to march, nor abide any longer upon the journey:
we saw it farre off and it appeared like a white church towre of
an exceeding height. There falleth over it a mightie river which
toucheth no part of the side of the mountaine, but rusheth over

the top of it, and falleth to the ground with a terrible noyse and clamor, as if 1,000 great belles were knockt one against another. I think there is not in the world so strange an overfall, not so wonderful to behold. Berreo told me it hath diamonds and other precious stones on it, and that they shined very farre off: but what it hath I knowe not, neither durst he or any of his men ascende to the toppe of the saide mountaine, those people adjoyning beeing his enemies and the way to it is so impassible.

But Mount Roraima first captured the imagination of the world at large during the last century when the illustrious explorer Sir Robert Schomburgk reached the bottom of this elevated plateau after an arduous trek lasting several months. He then discovered that the 'legendary' mountain of the Amerindians did actually exist, in the form of a huge sandstone mesa surrounded by cliffs which were over 1,000 feet in height. The Indians revered the mountain, calling it the 'Mother of Waters' as, indeed, it is; they believed that no white man would ever see it, for it found protection in an almost perpetual cover of rain cloud. When the average rainfall is eventually recorded, it is likely that the northern side of the mountain will prove to be one of the wettest places on earth.

In 1834 Schomburgk was engaged by the British Government to survey and establish the border between British Guiana, as Guyana then was, and Venezuela. For more than sixty years Britain had been wrangling with Venezuela over disputed territory, and some kind of settlement was imperative. Venezuela claimed all the land as far as the Essequebo River. Great Britain, successors to the Dutch, claimed all that the Dutch had possessed and the Dutch territory had never been properly defined. The territory in dispute covered over 50,000 square miles – bigger than the whole of England.

Showing considerable zeal, Schomburgk set out to establish the frontier for his employer. Any doubts were resolved in favour of the British: he set up posts and blazed trees, marking them with the insignia of Great Britain. Needless to say, Schomburgk's survey deeply offended the Venezuelans and only served to ensure the boundary dispute kept boiling. In fact in the 1890s another boundary commission produced a report that ran to three octavo volumes, plus an atlas of seventy-six maps. Venezuela's case was contained in three volumes and an atlas, Britain's in an atlas and seven volumes. Four months later each party submitted a counter case. At the hearing, Venezuela's case was presented by an ex-President of the United States: General Benjamin Harrison. The opening speech for Great Britain was made by Sir Richard E. Webster, Attorney General, and lasted thirteen days; the Venezuelan counterpart triumphantly equalled this record.

Eventually, the tricky business was settled by arbitration. Neither country was entirely satisfied, but the settlement seemed a reasonable compromise. Venezuela gained full control of the mouth of the Orinoco, which was essential to that country but Roraima proved to be a keystone in the demarcation of the frontiers for three countries: Venezuela, Brazil, and Guyana, all met on the summit, yet that vital piece of Guyanese territory could not be reached from Guyana. When we planned our expedition, this was how matters stood; there was an acknowledged hope that we might succeed in climbing through the inhospitable rain forests of the north, up 1,200 feet of overhanging sandstone, to gain access, for the first time in history, to this inaccessible territory from Guyana itself.

The various boundary disputes may have generated much fury, but the travelling done in their pursuit obviously also fired the imagination. This is Schomburgk on his first view of the mystery peak:

Before sunrise and half an hour after, Roraima was beautifully clear, which enabled us to see it in all its grandeur. Those stupendous walls rise to a height of 1,500 feet. They are as perpendicular as if erected with a plumb-line; nevertheless in some parts they are overhung with low shrubs which, seen from a distance give a dark hue to the reddish rock. Baron von Humboldt observed that a rock of 1,600 feet of perpendicular height has been sought for in vain in the Swiss Alps, nor do I think that Guiana offers another example of that description. A much more remarkable feature of this locality, however, lies in the cascades, which fall from their enormous height, and, strange as it may appear, afterwards flow in different directions into three of the mightiest rivers of the northern half of South America, namely the Amazon, the Orinoco, and the Essequibo ... for these wonderful cascades Roraima is famed among the Indians who in their dances, sing of the wonders of 'Roraima, the red rock, wrapped in clouds, the ever fertile source of streams'. I can imperfectly describe the magnificent appearance of these mountains. They convey the idea of vast buildings and might be called Nature's forum.

John William Burgon's 'Petra' might almost be a poetic expression of Schomburgk's first impressions of Roraima:

> Match me such marvel save in Eastern clime,
> A rose-red city half as old as Time.

Mo and Mike left for Georgetown in the last week of September via Luxemburg and Barbados – the cheapest flight we could organize. Mike, just back home, hardly had time to change his clothes and departed wearing a white suit and a somewhat archaic pair of sneakers, used to their detriment in the Himalayan foothills. He also sported several days' growth of beard and this made him look like a cross between an anthropologist on location (which he would shortly be), a beachcomber, and a colonial who had seen better days. Their short stay in Luxemburg proved expensive as Mo lost a wallet containing about seventy pounds. At the time the impact of the disaster was negligible: they were well insulated against worldly considerations by vast quantities of Dunkle Beer. In Barbados, Mike's smart white suit suffered further insult en route; a stray dog came along and pissed on it while he was swimming. Thereafter, the riff-raff of our four-legged friends paid Mike considerably more attention than normal politeness demanded!

Their first job on arrival in Guyana was to contact Adrian Thompson who owns a farm near Timehri airport, about twenty miles from Georgetown. Here all the expedition equipment was being collected and sorted out. Mo and Mike were to be kept busy packing food into kit bags each containing twenty-four man-days. When this was done they would go on ahead of the main party. On 1 October the remaining six expedition members left Heathrow, grossly overweight with camera equipment and the two Hilti bolt guns. We left London at 10 a.m. By 10 p.m. we were back in London, having spent most of the day in Luxemburg.

By the curious logic of the Atlantic agreement we were actually saving the expedition about £1,000 by travelling this way, as one can't take a cheap Caribbean flight direct from the United Kingdom.

We arrived in Guyana in the small hours of the morning. The air was moist and sticky, but a slight breeze was blowing out across the tarmac. I don't think any of us knew what to expect of Adrian Thompson: we knew he wasn't young, that he had something to do with the Guyana Government, and that he grew orchids. A tall bald-headed, distinguished man, very erect, came over to us:

'I'm Adrian Thompson. Welcome to Guyana.'

I introduced him to the others. True to his promise Adrian had our passage already cleared through the Customs and with little more than a cursory glance having been thrown at many thousands of pounds worth of equipment, we were hustled through to the awaiting vehicles. This in itself was nothing short of a miracle.

Adrian told us that Mo and Mike had already gone up country with most of the food and would save the rest of us time by opening up the trail to the cliff face. We, however, would not be able to get away for a couple of days. There was a meeting with the President lined up for us and also a number of receptions to be attended and various ministries to be visited. This last chore was Neil's to establish how the film was going to be made and how it was to be relayed from Roraima to Georgetown, and back to London for processing. This ensured that the film, once exposed, would be processed with the minimum delay so that rushes could be sent back to Georgetown for the Guyana Government to view. This would enable any technical corrections to be made by Alex in the field, and also keep the Guyana authorities happy, as they had suffered some embarrassing experiences with film units in the past (not the BBC) who seemed determined to portray the country as a backwater, seething with snakes and hostile Indians.

From our base at the Park Hotel, we soon realized that our expedition was creating a great undercurrent of excitement. It had an unusual amount of publicity throughout the country as well as overseas; people would stop us in the street and ask what we thought our chances were. Later on, we learnt that even the bookmakers were giving us poor odds!

There is a wonderfully rural air about Georgetown. I got the impression that, by living there for a few years, one would know everyone. Even the senior politicians are quite accessible, as we discovered when we walked down the street and entered the Residence of the President Chung. He wished us the best of luck in our venture and we received the first confirmation of our suspicions that there were political moves afoot when Adrian spoke.

'Sir, I have decided to send a radio signal back if we succeed in conquering Roraima. It will be "The sky is clear".'

'Very good, Adrian,' the President replied. 'And the best of luck.' I knew, however, that Mr Chung had more important things on his mind just then than the academic exercise of establishing access to Roraima's summit from Guyana. The rice crop was in jeopardy with the bad weather and he feared whether it would be harvested in time.

A couple of prospectors, or porknockers, were staying in the Park Hotel; these men had the lean, hard and drawn looks of men I had seen in New Zealand's west coast, men who had suffered hardships difficult for ordinary people to appreciate. Theirs is a tough life; panning for alluvial gold and diamonds. They are called porknockers because salted pork was their staple diet; when they had a run of bad luck, they used to borrow, or 'knock' pork from their more prosperous friends and be 'grubstaked'. The Government allows them to work in the interior territory, except for the area reserved for the Amerindians. One of the big centres for porknockers is Imbaimadi; Kamarang is also a prospecting centre and when I later met a Government mining official, he told me that some substantial finds were being made in that area. The gold and diamonds are purchased by buyers who frequently grubstake porknockers, and sold in Georgetown where a flourishing diamond cutting industry exists. Diamonds have a rather artificial market, however, which is strictly controlled internationally.

A great deal more work has still to be done on the geological history of Guyana. The basement rocks comprised of gneisses and schists which were intruded by granites are all greater than 2,000 million years old. These rocks were eroded down to an almost flat plain before rivers, coming from the east, brought in the vast sediments of the Roraima Formation. This formation, which has been described as 'the most spectacular and problematic geological phenomenon of the Guyana Shield' completely dominates the skyline between Colombia through Venezuela and Brazil and as far as Surinam, as its light grey to pinkish quartzilic sandstones and conglomerates form high ramparts which culminate in Mount Roraima itself. These ancient sediments are only a little disturbed, dipping only up to three degrees to the south or south-west, but they have been extensively intruded by thick gabbroic sills that have baked and silified the sandstones so that, near intrusions, they are now real quartzites.

Had I known this before I went to the mountain, I wouldn't have made the mistake in estimating the bolt gun's performance; the rock on the face was much harder than we had ever anticipated.

The sandstones surrounding the escarpment have been slowly removed by river erosion and, during the last few million years, the surrounding plains probably formed temporary shallow coastal seas, pierced by islands, but further earth movements during the last million years or so raised the whole land surface by some 400 feet, draining the seas and leaving sand and muds reaching up close to the foot of the escarpment.

In their book, *Continental Drift*, D. H. and M. P. Tarling find support for their theories of drift in the Roraima formation:

In and around Guyana this formation, more than half of which has been eroded away since its deposition over 1,000 million years ago, still covers over a million square kilometres and contains at least a million cubic kilometres of sediments which have been carried into South America from the north-east. The juxtaposition of Africa against South America offers an obvious source for these sediments and it is interesting to note that the diamonds, found at the bottom of the formation, get larger towards the Atlantic, while in West Africa similar rocks contain similar diamonds which continue to get larger towards their probable source in the Sudan.

One evening Booker Brothers, the large international company who had helped us obtain foodstuffs in Guyana, threw a big party for us. There I met the Postmaster General, J. A. Charles, a solidly built man who possessed great self-assurance, and we attempted to compromise over the question of first day covers. Although he promised to try and give us a percentage of the profit, he was obviously annoyed that the initiative for them had come from Britain. At the party I also met Mr George Bishop, the General Manager of Bookers. He had appeared at Everest Base camp whilst I was up at Camp

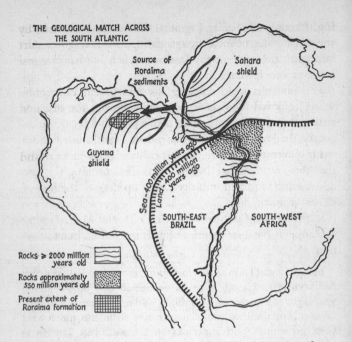

Source of
Roraima
sediments

Sahara
shield

Guyana
shield

Sea – 400 million years ago
Land – 400 million years ago

SOUTH-EAST
BRAZIL

SOUTH-WEST
AFRICA

Rocks ⩾ 2000 million years old

Rocks approximately 550 million years old

Present extent of Roraima formation

Five the previous year. He is an avid Himalayan wanderer and was already talking about his next trip – that autumn – again to the Everest region.

'You know, Hamish,' Adrian said to me one morning. 'You've earned great fame amongst the Amerindians already. They think your boiler suit idea is the funniest thing they've heard in years. It's said that you'll be cooked like a curassow [a turkey-like bird] by the time you reach Roraima.' As it happened, the ill-fated boiler suits had not arrived at Neil's office at the BBC in time, so they were sent on by BOAC; they had caught us up and now lay in the Customs Office within the GPO, despite Neil's endeavours to have them released: there they lie still, I presume, to this day. However, I had a spare suit amongst my personal gear so I wouldn't have to disappoint the Indians.

I watched Don unpacking his clothing. He had a fascinating selection of colourful apparel, obviously influenced by the trendy international golf scene. One garment – a shirt which he held up – was utterly fantastic; it had vertical multi-coloured stripes in bright ripstop nylon, like a multi-coloured bull's eye. I collapsed in a paroxysm of laughter when I saw it and it was some minutes before I'd recovered sufficiently to ask him what on earth it was.

'A shirt, of course,' he replied, rather hurt. 'Like it?'

I told him it might suit a rider in the Grand National, and dissolved into a further fit of laughter.

'Aye, I thought you'd get a laugh at that. You've no sense of taste,' he retorted huffily. 'That's the trouble with you teuchters: you're so used to rain, bog and mist, that you go mad at the first hint of a bit of colour! My trousers aren't so gay, though. Audrey ran them up on the machine for me,' he held up an array of brightly coloured trews; they had drawcord waists, cunningly designed to permit even the most optimistic reduction of his famous girth!

'I suppose you'll be wearing your bonny kilt. You can wear your boiler suit underneath to stop the spiders getting at your sporran!'

During this period, after a number of meetings with the Government departments, an agreement was eventually reached between the BBC and the Guyana officials. This stated that a certain number of film prints were to be supplied to the Guyana authorities; that we were not permitted to film Indian villages, and that a representative of the Government would accompany us: Maurice Barrow, the son of a Government minister. In addition, we would be accompanied by Mike Atherley, a Lieutenant in the Guyana Defence Force, and a wireless operator, Corporal Chaman Prasad. Not only were we encumbered with these individuals – sourly known to us as the spies – but Adrian insisted in taking along the son of a friend of his: Jonathan Wilkins. Adrian wanted him to do photographic work in connection with the flora. We had already received a somewhat high-handed letter from Jonathan before leaving the United Kingdom, asking what arrangements he could make as a freelance photographer and what type of film, etc., would be supplied by the expedition. I had immediately replied that the *Observer* had world newspaper and magazine rights and that there wouldn't be enough free film for expedition members. Jonathan drove a mini-moke with Greek lettering emblazoned upon it. He could, Adrian tried to pacify us, help with the transport.

Don put our feelings very concisely when he demanded fractiously, 'How much flotsam's going on this trip, anyhow?'

'Well, our two scientific members were always scheduled to come with us,' replied Adrian a shade defensively. 'But I wasn't expecting Maurice or the Lieutenant. Still, the Lieutenant will be useful at any rate, they're good lads in the Guyana Defence Force.'

'I suppose we'll need to have a wireless operator,' said Joe. We were all sitting in the lounge drinking rum and lime. 'He'll be quite handy for bringing the helicopter in when the weather is suitable, and for any airdrops we want.'

Our two scientists were Mike Tamessar and Ragu Prasad.

Mike Tamessar was our zoologist; a distinguished looking man of about forty, from Indian stock and a quietly confident, easy way with him. He admitted he was not too fit but, as he pointed out, he was to be taken in by helicopter if the conditions were suitable. He, Adrian and Ragu Prasad, our botanist, would be lifted to the summit to continue their collections. Ragu was a most likeable man; he, too, was of Indian descent with a roly-poly Friar Tuck sort of gait. He always looked untidy and he had a most engaging honest and open way with him.

'My good man!' he would say. 'I hope I done have to walk far; a'm not fit maan!'

Mike Atherley seemed initially to be a reserved, deep-thinking chap, obviously a professional soldier, who looked both fit and efficient. He would be an asset to any expedition. I personally thought it quite fair that he should come along; after all, on expeditions in places like Nepal, there is usually a liaison officer – who more often than not proves a liability – and the expedition generally has to pay his wages and supply him with equipment and food. Our two Guyana Defence Force men would be taken care of by the Government, as would Maurice Barrow. The two scientists would be paid for by a grant from their departments and also from a further grant which Adrian received from the Royal Botanical Gardens, Kew.

I first met Maurice 'the Spy' when we were assembled at the airport, waiting for our flight by GDF Islander aircraft to Kamarang, which was the nearest airstrip to Roraima. Maurice struck me as a typical arts graduate. He has frizzy hair and a light, almost fragile frame. This impression proved to be correct, he had obtained leave of absence from his college to come on the expedition. Though he had been thrust upon us in an apparently impromptu gesture by the Government we learned later from a slip of his tongue that he had actually been tipped off about his participation in the expedition about a month beforehand. Anyhow, we thought it was a small price to pay for all the cooperation which we were promised by the Guyana Government.

Chapter 4

For the Lord Thy God bringeth thee into a good
land; a land of brooks and water, of fountains,
and depths that spring out of valleys and hills.

Deuteronomy 8:7

Don, Joe and I went on the first flight, together with camera-
man Alex Scott. Our pilot was Major Chan-A-Sue, a somewhat plump engaging man who seemed entirely unperturb-
able. He had a deceptively casual way with him, common in
pilots used to dangerous mountain and jungle flights. Under
his experienced eye everything was checked, particularly
the payload, with the minimum of fuss.

'You guys want to see Roraima? We've got enough fuel for
the extra distance.'

'Sure, if the weather's okay,' said Joe.

'Well, we'll give it a go.'

We rose swiftly above the forest and looked down on
Georgetown with its uniform criss-cross streets running down
to the Demerara River. The Atlantic, grey in the early light,
took a darker tinge where it touched the coastline. There the
great rivers deposit their muddy silt forming ugly, dirty
beaches; literally black tide-marks. Presently we were flying
over the mighty Essequebo. That great expanse of slow-
moving water held a lurking threat in its vast, unharnessed
power, like a huge camoudi. Smaller rivers took tortuous
routes in an endeavour to reach the sea or their bigger
brothers, sometimes almost meeting again after mile long
loops of detour. Occasionally we saw an Indian paddling a
canoe, or a lonely shack thrown up in a small clearing on the
river bank.

Rivers are the motorways of the South American forests, but there are no navigable rivers passing close to Roraima, so visitors had to face a long journey, before the advent of air travel. First stages could be undertaken by canoe, but then it was by foot all the way, with food supplies an ever-increasing problem: most of it had to be carried in since the scattered native villages were so poor that they could only support small amounts of cassava and other basic essentials. The majority of the early travellers went in by the Rupununi in the south or, alternatively, by the Mazaruni from the north. Part of the southern approach is across savannah country; relatively easy walking. The northern side is a different kettle of fish: dense bush and forest country and rivers which swell overnight to become raging torrents, flooding large areas of forest in a matter of hours.

This was why travellers like Schomburgk, Appun, Barrington-Brown, Edgington and Flint were often forced to turn back through lack of provisions. A journey through the Rupununi savannahs could take eighteen days. In 1878 two men, McTurk and Boddam-Wetham, reached the mountain by way of the Mazaruni River and the savannahs of the west and almost reached the southern cliffs. They also saw, from a distance, the north face. They concluded that the prospect of reaching the summit was impossible, while the northern face, which is covered in dense forest, they considered unapproachable.

During the period 1879–84, a keen ornithologist called Henry Whitley visited the Roraima area:

The savannah land at the foot of Roraima is covered with immense boulders and smaller pieces of sandstone. These have evidently at some remote time broken away from the face of the rocks and although I made inquiries amongst all the old Indians some of whom had been in the service of Sir Robert Schomburgk forty years ago, not one of them had ever seen a part of the rock break away, and they told me that they must have fallen away ages ago, for they have no record of any such circumstance from the tales of their ancestors ...

The scenery round Roraima is very grand; rain was constantly falling on Roraima and Kukenaam during the greater part of my stay in the neighbourhood, and for days together the mountains were enveloped by clouds; at times, when it cleared, waterfalls were observed coming over the edge of the cliff, and when the sun was shining, the deep red colour on parts of the vertical sides, standing out as they did from the sombre coloured forest on the lower slopes, was seen to great advantage. It seems impossible to ascend either Kukenaam or Roraima except by balloon and this could only be done from the south side, on account of the strong wind constantly blowing from that direction. It might be possible to ascend by forming scaffolding, making use of the timber of the large forests on the slopes, but in this case it would be the work of great time and expense.

Whitely reached the foot of the cliff at 7,000 feet and reported that some distance along from his approach, the vertical cliff had fallen away and formed a sloping ledge. He must have had a good mountaineering eye, as this was found to be the only feasible line up the mountain until, eighty-eight years later, we climbed the Prow.

Flying over this part of Guyana, anything else is totally eclipsed by the rain forest; green on every point of the compass. The canopy undulated like a green sea, spreading outwards with an almost hypnotic monotony. Only the rivers broke the uniformity. Flying over this sort of terrain can be dangerous. If a plane crashes, especially a small one, it is enveloped in the forest and is almost impossible to spot from the air. Before leaving home, we ourselves had received a sad plea from the wife of a Georgetown hotel undermanager who had just returned to Scotland nine weeks after her husband's plane had disappeared on a flight to the Kaieteur falls. Her last desperate hope was that we might spot the plane. Unfortunately, the South American jungles have a long history of plane crashes occurring in remote regions where no trace is ever discovered of the victims. Men like Adrian, with experience of these rain forests, always carry a small flight bag of essentials – the size of a lady's handbag – containing a compass, some chocolate and snake-bite kit. It is obviously a sound precaution.

We were soon in cloud, flying almost blind, and Alex, who was sitting beside me, was worried about having enough daylight to film, because he had worked out that less than one per cent of the light falling on the forest canopy actually reached the ground below.

'Hey, you guys,' Chan-A-Sue shouted back to us above the roar of the engines. 'Roraima's straight ahead. You can just pick out the outline through the rain cloud.'

We peered through the murk to see a vertical wall rising endlessly into the cloud above; below the country had changed. There were wooded hills and abrupt escarpments now: the old coastline. Soon we emerged from the heavy cloud as we veered round to the western side of the mountain. Here the terrain changed again to the fine, rolling, bare hills of the Gran Sabana of Venezuela.

Despite the numerous descriptions we had read by now, that first flight we took over the mountain was fascinating. It had a mystic quality about it, with towers rising up in the swirling mist and tantalizing glimpses of deep ravines straight out of *Kubla Khan*.

We were all busy taking photographs and trying to identify some definite landmark, but to no avail. On the Guyana side the cloud cover was too thick and though it was interesting to see the mountain from the 'easy' side, it was not what we had wanted. Chan-A-Sue flew in as close as he dared but we only caught fleeting glimpses of overhanging reddish rock and waterfalls of amazing beauty.

I quoted Genesis exuberantly to Alex. 'Let the waters under the heavens be gathered together in one place . . .'

'Why don't you pull the chain on that rubbish o' Rabbie Burns?' Don turned round and grinned: 'Some nice wee slimy overhangs for you doon there, Jock.'

'I leave any of that simple rock work to my apprentice, Mr Brown, here,' I retorted.

'It'll be just like climbing on snow and ice on that stuff,' observed Joe in his usual humorous way. 'You'll be able to kick steps in the slime for me to follow.'

We knew Mo and Mike must be somewhere below us but the rain forest is like a great wet sponge, soaking up sound as well as water. We learnt later that they never heard our plane, yet we must have flown almost overhead.

We had to stop and refuel at an airstrip on the Brazilian border. Chan-A-Sue had trouble in finding the lonely airfield. He followed the course of a river and eventually, alongside a great cataract there lay the rough dirt strip. It was stifling hot; the country was open and the sun bounced off the dusty brown earth. Chan-A-Sue taxied over to a small army encampment where the soldiers filled our tanks from fuel barrels.

'Any chance of getting fresh food?' the Lieutenant in charge inquired. 'We've had nothing but tinned stuff for weeks now.'

'I'll see what I can do,' promised Chan-A-Sue. 'But you've no freezer, have you?'

'No, sir, no power here!'

There are many similar outposts in the country, where the soldiers – like the porknockers – exist miles from civilization, although in radio contact with their base.

When we landed at Kamarang, we realized it was a slightly larger place; there was a school and a police station, and the airstrip had regular flights to and from Georgetown. The runway was rough, typical of the remote country airstrips, but for a pilot of Chan-A-Sue's calibre, even the mini strips were child's play. Kamarang strip was also dusty and hot; it lay on the spit of land between the Mazaruni and the Kamarang rivers which meet at this point. A Government store was frequented by the porknockers and local residents. It stocked most things, when available, but just then goods were in very short supply and there was a local crisis over the shortage of foodstuffs.

'Porknockers can't operate without food!' one old sourdough muttered as he came out into the glare of the sun.

There is a cinema in Kamarang and also a health clinic but, generally speaking, the Amerindians in the region are a healthy people. Malaria is almost stamped out now, although effective control is difficult as there are still a number of migrating Indians who come over the border from Brazil; in the region of Amazonas it is still quite common. Stomach troubles are frequent, however; these are attributed to over-hot peppers and casiri, the popular fermented drinks. As with many other native communities in isolated regions, epidemic influenza is fairly widespread and nearly everyone on the expedition was affected at some stage. Snake bites are treated with Crotalidae Antivenin.

The others had arrived at Kamarang before us; a great pile of equipment was neatly stacked in the army compound. It had a Robinson Crusoe atmosphere with the palm and pau pau trees, and some parrots which had been caught by the soldiers and were quite tame. There was also a pet curassow. At the other end of the clearing in which the corrugated roofed huts were placed, and beyond a somewhat isolated hut on which the unnecessary sign 'Shithouse' hung, was a rough jetty to which several canoes were moored. Part One Orders, conspicuously pinned to a tree, had a ruling as to when firearms could be used whilst on guard duty; one permissible occasion was: 'For the killing of tigers for self protection.' 'Tigers' covers all the cat family found in Guyana, but the jaguar in this district are quite large. We found the rest of the expedition under an open-sided hut which constituted the dining room: a table was centrally placed with long boards to either side which served as seats. We joined them in a short snack and learned that Adrian had had to remain in Georgetown for another day to attend to some urgent business. With a casual 'cheerio' and a wave, Chan-A-Sue sauntered back to his Islander and climbed aboard. We were later to be deeply grateful to this unassuming man for saving our expedition.

It had been decided that Don, Joe and I, the three climbers, should occupy one canoe whilst the rest of the party travelled in the other which was slightly faster. This meant that the camera crew would be more mobile; they could film us, let us pass by, then catch up again. Neil was in his element, eagerly suggesting shots that Alex might take as we loaded the canoes.

The river stole sulkily past like heavy beer slowly leaking from a brewery in vast quantities; we cast off from the large fallen tree which served as a jetty. The water was dark brown and lush vegetation overhung the banks. We were off at last, though not free from the distractions of civilization for the roar of the powerful outboards destroyed any tranquillity there might be and ensured that our only glimpses of wild life would be from a great distance.

We circled the spit of land and made our way up the Mazaruni, a large river just as dark as the Kamarang and both quiet and peaceful in this section. The scenery was new to me, though it reminded Don of the Amazon, down which he had been on a raft with a mutual friend, Dave Bathgate, of Edinburgh, who was later on Everest with us. Don considered it hadn't really been a strenuous trip.

It was much cooler on the water. Our canoe was making a steady nine knots, held to the side of the river by its 'skipper', whilst Neil's canoe darted to and fro like a wild thing with its fifty h.p. outboard. On several occasions we narrowly missed swamping one another. Then it started to rain. It wasn't just heavy rain, it seemed to slant down into the water like welding rods. In a trice we were soaked through and I started to bale with an old tin can. Joe and Don were sitting in front on a pile of kit bags, so they couldn't reach down to the bottom of the canoe to help me. Monotonously, I filled and emptied that ancient milk tin and mused over our plans. I was doubtful about the chances of the helicopter I'd so cleverly persuaded Adrian to hire to ferry our food and equipment.

I have had considerable experience flying in helicopters in bad conditions and I believed that conditions on Roraima were more than plain bad – they would be a pilot's nightmare. There would be tremendous turbulence round the cliffs, we had already experienced some that day when Chan-A-Sue flew close in to the towering sandstone, and a small helicopter . . . This was no sudden misgiving: while at home I had contacted a friend of mine, Ted Nowak, one of the most experienced helicopter pilots in Britain, and had voiced my doubts about the feasibility of a small chopper reaching the top of Roraima. He had amplified my misgivings and went so far as to say that it would be unlikely to reach 9,000 feet with any payload at all, unless it was supercharged. The one we were relying on wasn't, of course, but according to Adrian, the owner, George Gransoult, was himself a pilot and thought that to supply equipment to El Dorado swamp at the bottom of the Wall would present no trouble whatsoever. I don't think that any of us at this stage realized just how bad the conditions could be at Roraima except Adrian, who knew the seriousness of the weather, but he knew little about the limitations of helicopters. None of us could foresee the most crucial fact that the helicopter would be unserviceable at the time we most needed it!

Our plan was to walk to the El Dorado swamp, which was the final camp of the 1971 and the 1972 expeditions, with the minimum of equipment and supplies; there to await the first good day so that the helicopter could land with our equipment. We could radio to its base when conditions were suitable. Foolishly we banked on this, much against my better judgement. The helicopter was also to be used to transport the scientists and our honorary Postmaster to the summit in order to conduct their various duties.

Our destination that day was the village of Maiurapai. It was from this village that Adrian had arranged for the helicopter to be refuelled (aviation spirit would be transported by canoe from Kamarang by the Guyana Defence Force) and the main cache of our supplies would be dumped at this same village. Travelling in the canoe with us was one Bobby Fernandez, the son of wealthy parents from Georgetown; he had tired of city life and now led a somewhat footloose existence in the outback of Guyana, canoeing up remote rivers. He was to remain at Maiurapai to help the helicopter pilot. Bobby was obviously a very experienced man in the bush and he could handle a canoe like an Indian. He had a passion for swimming and, whenever he had a chance, his dark brown body would flash through the water like a caiman.

The driver of our boat was the headman of Kako village which lay up ahead of us, at the confluence of the Kako River and the Mazaruni. He wore a sphinx-like expression on his stern dignified face. He was known as the 'Skipper' and, as headman, he carried a lot of responsibility on his sturdy shoulders. I could hardly keep pace baling against the rain but he picked up another can to help me. After what seemed like many hours, he cut the engine abruptly and, through a solid curtain of rain, we ran gently on to a small sandbank. There were other slender canoes parked near by. He pointed up the bank to where we could see the top of a hut.

'Kako,' he explained, and jumped out nimbly. We straightened up painfully and tried to ease our cramped legs.

'Are we here?' asked Joe, pulling his cagoule hood drawcord for the fiftieth time.

'Buggered if I know,' muttered Don, speaking around a sodden cigarette. 'I don't think I've got my canoe legs, yet, though,' he straightened himself slowly, rocking the canoe.

Meanwhile, the faster boat had fallen behind; we presumed this must be due to engine trouble. We were showing little interest in the filming anyhow; our enthusiasm was, to say the least, dampened!

We staggered up the bank to the village like senior citizens en route to the post office to collect their pensions. The village was immaculate: neat, straight pathways linked the houses and the clearing was fringed with palm trees and bamboos. In the background were cultivated fields. There was a general air of prosperity. The houses, like all buildings in that part of the world, stood on stilts made from the wonderful hardwood which grows so profusely everywhere, and were thatched with palm leaves. We were ushered into a small hut where we took off our saturated clothes.

'It feels bloody cold here,' Joe stood shivering amidst a pool of water which had just drained off his person.

'Yes, you wouldn't think we were only a short way from the Equator would you?'

'I was told at school that it was an imaginary line,' said Don, performing a miracle by lighting another fag. 'Bloody imaginary, if you ask me!'

Healthy, cheerful kids peered out of hut doorways at us as we stood in the bare, open-sided hut, watching the deluge. I risked another quotation as I looked out: 'The same day were all the fountains of the great deep broken up, and the windows of heaven were opened.'

'You know you're not in the right vocation,' said Joe ironically. 'You should have been a lay preacher.'

Speaking of religion, the inhabitants of Kako were Seventh Day Adventists, but a lot of people in this area are followers of that nineteenth-century Brazilian phenomenon, the Halleluya religion, brought back by a Macusi Indian called Itanchichiwon who had been taken to England by some missionaries and eventually returned to his native land to hand on a very Victorian mixture of evangelical piety and prohibitions which nevertheless conquered the local witch doctors and continued to make converts down to the present day in the depths of the South American rain forest.

'This rain's worse than Wales,' I remarked to Joe who was peering out under the door of our hut.

'Or Glencoe,' he retorted smartly.

At that moment the skipper came charging along the path wearing a dry set of clothing; a vain precaution since, during the short sprint he made from a near-by hut, they became as waterlogged as the ones he had just discarded.

'We go up to Maiurapai,' he informed us, pointing up river. 'Other boat go past.'

I continued baling wearily as the banks of the river grew inky black. Dusk fell with a startling suddenness. Each of us seemed in a trance as the rain beat down and we huddled there, wrapped up in our thoughts and trying to keep the driving water from getting inside the hoods of our anoraks.

Suddenly the motor cut; we had arrived at Maiurapai. We drifted in towards the true right bank. Again it was a log for a pier and we saw shadowy figures there on the steep muddy bank. A pile of kit bags were lying at the bottom of the slope. From the grunts above and repeated curses we realized that the equipment was being ferried up. Even in the rain, fireflies – some of remarkable intensity – flickered and moved to and fro.

The others had already made several trips. Neil told us later he was in the bows as they landed and dropped his waterproof torch into the depths of the river. He was so wet anyhow that he had just plunged straight in after it. It was only once he was submerged that he thought of all the charming creatures which inhabit the inland waterways of Guyana, from sting rays to piranha and orifice fish. (The last mentioned were particularly feared as they have the endearing habit of entering one's urethra in search of uric acid. They are barbed one way fish and don't come down again.) However, he needn't have worried for most of the rivers in that particular area were fairly safe for swimming.

It took us about an hour to ferry the kit bags up that steep, slippery slope. We carried them by torchlight to the huts on the fringe of a small savannah at the top and dumped them inside the largest one. It was on stilts and had no floor other than one or two hand-sawn boards. It was to be our bedroom for the next two nights. Some of the company made use of a couple of small thatched huts near by.

With quiet efficiency, the skipper slung his hammock at the far end of this unfinished hut whilst the rest of us – Neil, Don, Bobby Fernandez and I disposed ourselves upon the hand-sawn boards. Don and I slept alongside each other, Neil and Bobby found a similar plank on the other side on which to pass a somewhat perilous night.

'Any chance of creepy-crawlies here, Bobby?' I inquired a shade nervously as I had just caught a glimpse of a bat flitting past in the torch beams, and my thoughts immediately flew to Dr McInnes Fletcher's book and the Desmodus rotundus.

'Don't know, man,' he said. 'But I'm buggered if I'm going to fix up anything else tonight.'

I was of much the same opinion, my resistance utterly beaten down by the constant hammering of the rain during the ninety mile canoe trip.

After years of practice – on expeditions and in the bush – I have become highly proficient at securing the best place to lodge my carcase for a night's rest. It is therefore somewhat disconcerting to meet another who is equally adept: Don, for example! It's like playing a game of chess with him. That night I had promptly dropped my wet rucksack on the best plank, to 'book it', so to speak, knowing full well that I could turn it over on to its dry side as it wasn't nailed to the joists running across the hut. Don went a stage further, however, and sat on the board, thereby establishing a stronger priority. That night he had the best board, without a doubt, but we were all so tired that we dropped into a deep sleep, even in our damp sleeping bags.

Chapter 5   There was naught to rouse their anger; yet the
             oath that each one swore
             Seemed less fit for publication than the one that
             went before.

             'Bastard from the Bush', *Henry Lawson*

I was awakened by rain – heavy rain – beating down on the
corrugated iron roof, but it soon cleared and I propped myself up on one elbow to look over the low boarding which
formed a wall behind Don. I could see open savannah with
rain forest beyond; in the distance, the trees seemed to rise
until they blended with the low cloud.

We had had nothing to eat the previous night and were
ravenous.

'Well, I must go and hunt for some grub, Neil,' I remarked
brightly. He had just stuck his head out of his sleeping bag
and wore that baffled look which we all have from time to
time, wondering where the hell he was. He gave a groan
and groped blindly in his rucksack – which served as a pillow
– for a fag.

'Smoke, Don?' he asked sleepily.

'Aye, thanks,' Don caught the cigarette deftly as it spiralled
towards him. He was sitting up now.

'There's some chocolate in this kit bag here, Hamish. Do
you want some?' Neil asked as he pulled out a slab of Dairy
Milk.

'Great, thanks.'

'Want some, Bobby?' he shouted across.

'Thanks man,' said Bobby. (Everything is 'man' in
Guyana.)

Neil had heard from the Indians that this was a bad place

for jiggers, who like dry, sandy areas close to human habitation. These pertinacious creatures burrow into the skin of the lower leg or the foot or, worse still, under the toe-nails, and excavate quite a fair-sized cavity. They then take up temporary residence there and lay a large number of eggs. All this causes considerable irritation though when the infected area becomes 'high' they can be eradicated by someone with a good eye and a steady hand using a needle; or one can use ether or alcohol. It is quite common to collect a hundred or more of these creatures about one's person.

The 1971 expedition had had trouble with them when they parachuted in. They had even had plans to parachute on to the top of Mount Roraima. We all agreed that was definitely not for us and spent an agreeable half hour swopping horror stories of various intrepid aviators who had launched themselves on to or off various of the world's high places and the unhappy landings they had experienced.

Later that day, when the sun was beating down, we had our first good view of Roraima, twenty-five miles to the south, rising out of its green carpet rather like a huge table. But the view was disappointingly brief as it was soon enveloped in mist again.

The all-out bid which was to conquer the summit of Roraima in 1884 was financed by the Royal Geographical Society, the British Association and the Royal Society. These august bodies put their money behind Harry I. Perkins, assistant Crown Surveyor and Everard im Thurm (later Sir Everard) who was a magistrate at Maccassema on the upper Pomeroon River. When they arrived on Roraima they joined forces with an orchid collector named Siedal.

Perkins's party left the Essequebo and paddled up the Potaro River until they were one day's journey above the Kaieteur Falls where the main river plunges over a lip of Kaieteurian sandstone in a sheer hypnotic drop of 741 feet, and is one of the really great sights in the world.

Perkins's destination above the Falls was the old mission of Chinebowie. They arrived on 8 November but did not resume their journey until 14 November, as some of their baggage was delayed. This was the start of their long walk to Roraima, through dense and monotonous rain forest to the south-west. The party – like most travellers in similar environments – found it singularly depressing. As Everard im Thurm wrote in an account in *Timehri* (the Journal of the Royal Agricultural and Commercial Society of British Guyana, June 1885) which was later published in his collection of papers: *Thoughts, Talks and Tramps*, in 1934:

Thus, on this fourth morning of our journey through the forest life seemed to me as gloomy as it could possibly be: the difficulties which lay before us seemed insurmountable; success seemed impossible.

So it was for the first few hours of our walk that morning. Then suddenly, at about 10 a.m., the forest ended in a distinct line and the path passed out of the forest on to the wide open savannah – and such a glorious savannah! It ran along the ridges of the mountains, down its slopes, over wide, well watered and green plains, up on to other ranges of curiously terraced mountains, and on, ever over mountain after mountain, until it lost itself, to our eyes, in the blue misty distance . . .

From out of the long black prison of the gloomy forest, a step had brought us into this splendidly wide world with its atmosphere of freedom and welcome promise of success.

They joined forces with Siedal at the base of the Roraima cliffs:

By a lucky chance, on the day of our arrival the mountain was fairly free from cloud; so that we saw a ledge, running diagonally from the bottom to the top of the opposite cliff of Roraima, which, from where we were, certainly seemed to offer a very practicable way of ascent. Yet, knowing that of the few other than Indians who had visited Roraima and had pronounced its summit inaccessible almost all had tried to attack it from the very point at which we now were, we failed to persuade ourselves that our ledge was really practicable. And only at one other point on this face of Roraima did it seem in the least possible even to think of attempting an ascent; and this second point afforded but the very smallest gleam of hope ...

After due examination, it appeared that there would be especially three points of possible difficulty to be met in making an ascent by the ledge. In the first place that part of the forest slope which we should have to pass before reaching the foot of the ledge had, as we then thought, never been penetrated by man and was of quite unusual density ...

But a second difficulty, evident from below, was presented in the fact that the lower part of the ledge seemed much broken, and indeed appeared to be not so much a continuous shelf but rather a shelf which had at some time been broken up into large masses of rock, which, towering over the forest, looked formidable enough from below ...

But the most doubtful point of all was where, some two thirds of the length of the ledge, a considerable stream of water fell on to it from the summit of Roraima. This stream, falling on the ledge, had eaten away, and made a deep gap, impenetrable to the eye from below, in its surface. It certainly appeared that this might well be impassable; and our only hope was that we might just possibly be able to climb down into it, and up its further side and so on to the upper part of the ledge, which from that point to the summit of the mountain seemed accessible enough ...

We found that the path (to the foot of the ledge) had been cleared only just sufficiently to allow us to pass, and that not without considerable difficulty ... Seldom if ever did we step on the real ground, but instead we climbed, hands and feet all fully employed, over masses of vegetation dense enough to bear our weight, over high-piled rocks and tree stumps and not seldom under boulders of vast size, up tree trunks and along tree branches, across the beds of many streams so filled with broken rocks that the water heard trickling below was unseen. Nor did the dense and universal coating of moss, filmy ferns and lungworts afford any but the most treacherous foothold and handhold ...

It should perhaps before have been explained that what had appeared from below the broken part of the ledge really consists of three rounded spurs, or shoulders, running from a little way up the cliff down on to the ledge; and that these spurs are all wooded, though not so densely as the ground below the ledge, while in parts a few huge boulders stand out over the tree tops ...

The way, which was very difficult and wearisome though at no point dangerous, was again over, under and along more tree-roots, branches and trunks, again over, under and along more rocks and boulders, and over and up steep slopes of wet slippery mud – tree, rock and mud being alike wrapped in the usual covering of wet moss. Over such ground as this we made our way round the three spurs, and at last came in sight of the part of the ledge on to which falls the stream from above. A fairly gentle slope, covered with coarse grass, taller than ourselves, led down, for a considerable distance, to the actual point on to which the water fell, which, to our great delight, we saw was no deep impassable pool or ravine, but a broad, sloping reach of broken rocks; on the other side of this, the ledge sloped almost as gradually upward, but this upward slope consisted for some distance of a slippery expanse of rock, broken by faintly marked step-like ledges, over the whole of which in the heavy rainy season a continuous flood of water must pour, but which was now almost dry. At last the way to the top lay before us clear, and, if somewhat difficult, certainly passable ...

Up this part of the slope we made our way with comparative ease ... Then the step was taken – and we saw surely as strange a sight, regarded simply as a product of nature, as may be seen in this world; nay it would probably not be rash to assert that very few sights even as strange can be seen. The first impression was one of inability mentally to grasp such surroundings; the next that one was entering on some strange country of nightmares for which an appropriate and wildly fantastic landscape had been formed, some dreadful and stormy day, when, in their mid career, the broken and chaotic clouds had been stiffened, in a single instant, into stone. For all around were rocks and pinnacles of rocks of seemingly impossibly fantastic forms, standing in apparently fantastic ways – nay placed one on, or next to, the other in positions seeming to defy every law of gravity – rocks in groups, rocks standing singly, rocks in terraces, rocks as columns, rocks as walls and rocks as pyramids, rocks ridiculous at every point with countless apparent caricatures of the faces and forms of men and animals, apparent caricatures of umbrellas, tortoises, churches, canons, and of innumerable other most incongruous and unexpected objects. And between the rocks were level spaces, never of great extent, of pure yellow sand, with streamlets and little waterfalls and pools and shallow lakelets of pure water; and in some places there were little marshes filled with low scanty and bristling vegetation. And here and there, alike on level space and jutting from some crevice in the rock, were small shrubs in form like miniature trees, but all apparently of one species. Not a tree was there; no animal life was visible or, it even seemed, so intensely quiet and undisturbed did the place look, ever had been there. Look where one would on every side it was the same; and climb what high rock one liked, in every direction, as far as the eye could see was this same wildly extraordinary scenery.

And so the Lost World was conquered and nothing even faintly resembling a pterodactyl had been discovered.

Far from ending speculation about this remote mesa, the successful ascent only increased the interest, especially scientific interest, and many expeditions followed. Adrian Thompson, for example, had climbed the mountain twice before from the easier Venezuelan side. In the company of the 1963 Bangor Expedition, he also climbed the neighbour of Roraima – Kukenaam (8,600 feet). It covers roughly the same area as Roraima – twenty-five square miles – and, like the normal ascent up Roraima, the climb was little more than a scramble. According to John Ogden, a member of the party, the standard of the climb would be classed as 'moderate' (but strenuous) in Britain.

But the approach via the Guyanan northern side of Mount Roraima was virtually unknown, bastioned by some of the most daunting forest country in the world. In 1958, P. H. B. Bailey, of the British Guiana Geological Survey, succeeded in penetrating the Mazaruni River's drainage system by following the Waruma to the escarpment on the north-west side of the Prow. But no one, until the 1971 United Kingdom expedition led by Adrian Warren, had succeeded in getting up through the forest to the bottom of the Prow, the most northerly point of Roraima. Their expedition was strong and ambitious. It did a great deal of worth-while scientific study and had its fair share of drama besides. Their plans to climb the Prow of Roraima proved abortive, however; viewing the tremendous cliff, they realized that it would require a major endeavour to scale it. But they knew that Adrian Thompson, John Streetly and Bev Clark hoped to attempt the Prow in 1972, and took useful photographs and cine film of the face for them. This stood us in good stead when we were making our own plans for 1973.

Only a couple of families live at Maiurapai where we waited for the rest of our party. The hut next to ours was the home of Phillip, the hunter. A great old man, weather-beaten and kindly. Neil had arranged to film his family making cassava bread that day, but they mysteriously disappeared. We were told later that they felt so embarrassed, not being able to afford us hospitality, that they had moved on to another plot which they had down river.

The making of cassava bread from cassava roots is a fascinating process. Cassava is the staple food of tropical South America but it contains varying proportions of a cyanogenetic glucoside which readily breaks down to give prussic acid. One wonders how many people died before they found a safe way to use the plant. The acid must be extracted so the roots are first grated on special boards. These boards are made from a softwood into which four to five thousand small chips of stone are hammered, they are finished off with a mixture of vermilion paint and latex which binds the chips and gives the board a pleasant appearance. The coarse, moist meal is fed through a sieve to remove the larger flakes, after which the meal is poured into basket-work tubes which have loops at the bottom. The tubes are hung from the roof timbers; a pole is passed through the loop at the bottom of the tube and the tubes are squeezed until every drop of juice is removed. The meal, now almost dry, is put through a sieve once more and then baked on griddles as small mounds of bread. The juice is boiled and reboiled until all remnants of the deadly acid have been removed and is used as a preservative called 'cassareep' in the Indians' equivalent of scouse.

Joe went down to the landing with his new American telescopic fishing rod to see what the river could offer. I followed a little while later and was amused to see one of the Guyana Defence Force soldiers standing behind Joe, his sub-machine gun slung handily over his shoulder.

'Waiting for him to catch a big one?' I asked.

'No man, no big ones in here; no fish at all!' he grinned.

Joe has an insatiable curiosity. He will rummage about for hours catching insects and snakes, he is compelled to examine everything. While he was rooting in the undergrowth on the river bank, he cut his arms with razor grass; he looked as if he had just tried to force his way through a barbed-wire entanglement.

'There's no fool like an old fool,' was Don's sympathetic observation. 'I like to take things easy when I come into a new country. Let myself absorb things slowly and watch the native people. These buggers know what to do,' he pointed to one of the local Amerindians who was honing his cutlass. 'You don't see them sprinting after a bushmaster just for the hell of it!'

Joe retorted to the effect that you never learn if you don't have an inquiring mind, and drew my attention to a fantastic butterfly, pounding by like a flying telephone directory. It was certainly a great place for these aircraft and creepy-crawlies.

Chaman Prasad, the wireless operator, came over holding a note.

'Message from Mr Thompson,' he said. 'He is leaving Kamarang this morning and will be here tonight.'

This meant we would be able to get going up river in the morning. Chaman was a wonderful fellow. The longer we knew him, the nicer we found him. Nothing was too much trouble for him and he was always cheerful. He always managed to get through to his base somehow or other and his call sign 'Zero Delta' could be heard at all times of the day as he repeated it to the relay stations. It was arranged that once he moved up river he should have a relay station here at Maiurapai, manned by another operator of the GDF, which would then relay his messages to Kamarang. From there contact was easily established with Georgetown and GDF Headquarters where Major Joe Singh was coordinating all the military aspects of the expedition.

The two spies and Cham had their hammocks strung up in an open-sided shack which also served as cookhouse. Gordon and Alex had also managed to squeeze into this small area and their hammocks were strung parallel, nearly touching, so that they looked like white piglets. After our hurried bedding down of the previous night the rest of us, plus Joe, prepared our hammocks and slung them between the roof rafters in our hut. Dusk was not far away. Don sited his conveniently above the corner planks, defending his claim by saying that, as I was taller, I wouldn't have any trouble getting into mine.

Adrian arrived in the late afternoon and brought with him quite a lot of extra supplies and a number of Indian porters. As we ferried everything up from the landing, Alex and Gordon were busy filming. Isaac Jerry, an Amerindian, came with Adrian; he had accompanied him on many treks into the backwoods: if Adrian ever publishes accounts of these expeditions they will provide some of the most interesting travel literature available about the South American jungle.

Isaac is a short, very sturdily built man of middle age. His face is scarred and he walks, like Adrian, very erect. Though he was brought up in Georgetown, he returned to this area and now grows peanuts in the village of Jowala. He taught himself to read and write and has a vast knowledge of life in these remote regions. I can think of few more enjoyable evenings than lying in my hammock alongside Adrian and Isaac (as I did later on), listening to their tales.

After a good meal of stew we returned to our floorless hut for the night. This was to be my first night in a hammock: it certainly seemed a precarious undertaking! To climb into it involved balancing on the very edge of a loose plank and launching myself on to it whilst it swung like a pendulum; then endeavouring to get inside. Since my weight was bearing down on it, it was taut like a laid rope, so I had great trouble in forcing it open in order to climb inside. This farce was enacted about seven feet above the sandy ground into which were hammered some thin wooden stakes. I wondered uneasily if I would have this trouble throughout the expedition!

The arrangements for moving up river again were to be the same as before: the BBC personnel in one boat, the three of us and some Indians in the other. Adrian was going to follow us up later in the day.

'Got to get some good stuff in the rapids, lads,' Neil waxed enthusiastic. 'We turn off into the Waruma just a bit up the Kako and I must get some shots of you paddling and pushing the canoe up the rough stretches.'

'You know I've an aversion to water, Neil. I'd like to stay aboard,' I said firmly.

'Well, if you stay in, Don and Joe can always get out,' Neil suggested, glancing at Don apprehensively.

'Do you think this is a ruddy circus?' Don asked pointedly. He was nursing a sore instep, punctured by walking incautiously bare foot. 'I don't like water either – Joe's the aquatic rep. here.'

Joe was fortunately out of earshot at the time.

The weather was better now and we had a fine view of Roraima standing out clearly against the sky. Even from this distance the cliffs showed up bright red.

'See the angle of that Prow, Don?' I pointed. 'Overhangs the whole ruddy way.'

'Aye, it certainly looks as if we'll keep dry for a bit, at any rate,' he replied, looking from under a baseball type cap he was wearing.

We carried our gear down to the three canoes; they were smaller ones than before, as the large dugouts wouldn't be able to negotiate the shallower Waruma. We were refreshed after our short stay at Maiurapai and eager to get going again. There was an air of bustle now; Indians were running down to the landing with kit bags and several other canoes were tethered up at the bank. These were slender dugouts burned out of large tree trunks; their sides are widened by levering with huge clothespeg-like forked sticks on the walls whilst the canoe is heated over the coals of a fire. The canoes are very unstable and one must sit cautiously in them, in balance, with the minimum of movement. I felt as if I was riding a bicycle for the first time.

Chapter 6

Stood up to his waist in water,
To his armpits in the river,
Swam and shouted in the river,
Tugged at sunken logs and branches,
With his hands he scooped the sand-bars,
With his feet the ooze and tangle . . .

'Hiawatha's Sailing', *Longfellow*

We could still use outboards, as long as we watched out for the fallen trees which were swept down by the floods. The water level was two feet lower than the previous day. Isaac said that this was a disadvantage as it would shorten the distance we could navigate on the Waruma, which is a much smaller river than the Kako.

'I don't think we get 'em above Camp 1,' he said gloomily.

We hadn't really got to know the others yet. Jonathan was always hanging about. His Nikon camera clicked incessantly – not with our film, I should add. Maurice 'the Spy' had been told by his Government to film the expedition; he had no experience in using his borrowed Bolex, but Alex patiently helped him. Adrian and Isaac observed the great pile of BBC equipment with misgivings – especially Gordon's Nagra recorder and long unwieldy gunmike, which neither of them thought would survive very long. However, they had underestimated Gordon; that same microphone was returned intact to BBC Glasgow: Gordon had carried it as if it was a bottle of nitroglycerine.

We had made a pile of the equipment which was to be taken in to El Dorado swamp by helicopter on top of the planks inside the hut. Bobby, remaining in charge at Maiurapai, knew the order in which they were to be sent. Adrian informed us that the helicopter would be working in the district fairly soon as a mining company wanted to hire it at irregular intervals during the next few weeks. The pilot would therefore standby at Maiurapai with Bobby – provided we fed him – until he had a radio message from us to ask for a supply lift.

We had thus left most of our equipment to follow in this manner and packed the bare essentials for the walk in through the rain forest. Alex took only one camera with him, the Eclair, and left the large BL, most of the lenses and the small cine cameras still packed in their boxes which were stuffed full of silica gel in an attempt to prevent the humidity ruining them. We left enough food for Bobby and the pilot, but the GDF radio operator would have his food supplied from Kamarang.

I had already spoken to Isaac about finding runners to take back the *Observer* articles and the BBC rushes to the camp and he assured me that it would be no trouble.

The bulk of all this early organization had fallen on Adrian and Isaac's shoulders; we could do little to help as we were unfamiliar with the routine on such expeditions. But it was already apparent to us that things were not running smoothly. There was a conspicuous lack of food, and a shortage of porters and one mini crisis seemed to follow the next. Neil soon began to voice the unease which most of us felt.

We passed the insignificant mouth of the Paikwa River. The 1971 British expedition had made a survey of the lower stretches of this river and had considered it a possible access route to Roraima; but eventually they chose the Waruma instead, despite the four sets of rapids encountered before the river becomes impassable for canoes.

The canoe journey up the Kako and Waruma was quite enjoyable. Due to the aforementioned chaos we went ahead of the other canoes – despite Neil's pleas – and no filming was done in the lower Waruma. The rapids were not so impressive, after all. Even with my mistrust of water, I had few qualms. Although in one fast-flowing section where there were a lot of submerged logs, the motor kept fouling on the bottom and we were swung round in the current; we were only saved from capsizing by a tree overhanging the river bank.

This was real Colonel Fawcett stuff, with lianas hanging from the Mora trees, true Tarzan country. I told our fisherman, Joe, how the local people use chips from the Mora wood to poison fish. It sounded a bit faster than using the rod.

'Not exactly sport though, is it?' was his reply.

Normally the Indians use lengths of the roots and stems of the Lonchocarpus vine for fish poisoning. These are pounded until they turn to light yellow, evil-smelling fragments. When wicker baskets containing these roots are dipped into the water, a milky juice runs out from the pulverized plant and the fish become asphyxiated.

Below one dangerous set of rapids, the Indians asked us to get out and walk and join them farther upstream. The canoe was expertly guided in alongside a fallen tree trunk and Don put out a hand to hold the craft steady. An enormous spider – about five inches across – sat regarding him balefully, a few inches from where his hand grasped the branch.

'Aye, that is a nice welcome to the parlour,' he remarked drily.

One Indian came ashore with us and set off at speed through the riverain forest. The walking itself wasn't difficult, but there were plenty of streams to cross, some of them bridged by slippery tacoubas, or tree jams.

'Hey, where's the fire?' Don shouted presently from the rear. He doesn't walk fast normally and was handicapped now by his sore foot. It wasn't Joe in a hurry, though, but our Indian guide who weaved his way amongst the undergrowth like a dark shadow. The Amerindians have a reputation for moving too fast in their native environment for European parties. Certainly they do walk, and even run, very quickly indeed. We were to witness this on the return trip of the expedition when the Indians, carrying loads of over 100 lb., actually ran and we had the greatest difficulty in staying with them although our loads were virtually non-existent.

We rejoined the canoe in relatively still waters above the last section of rapids and once more forged our way up-stream; the 'lookout' in the bows shouting a warning when-ever he spotted a submerged log, and paddling furiously when we once again entered white water. The river widened gradually and the Indian in the bows pointed to a high bank where a rough clearing was visible; trees had been felled and now lay about in an untidy heap, rather like a spilt box of matches.

'Camp 1, sir.'

This was one of the camps which had been used by P. B. H. Bailey of the Department of Geological Survey for British Guiana. Because of the nature of its work, the camps were fairly close together. All that remained now was a partial clearing on the banks of the river.

The canoe was moored to a log and we climbed up a steep muddy slope and unloaded the gear. Indians already at the camp came down to help. The sun was shining and long rays of intense light angled down through the canopy be-hind the clearing, spot-lighting the chaos as if it were the stage-set of an earthquake.

The camp was simple; a couple of wooden frames made from the wonderfully straight saplings found in the forests, lashed together with strips of Kakarallis bark. These frames, covered with tarpaulins, afford the best type of shelter in the forest. Hammocks are slung between the two main sup-port poles, which are about six feet above the ground and form the two main longitudinal members of the 'hut'. In no time at all the Indians had taken our bright yellow p.v.c sheets and stretched them taut over the ridge and main frames. The sheets overlapped the sides of the frames where thin vertical poles, firmly staked into the ground, were in-serted into the eyelets. Kakarallis guys tensioned the whole frame, leading from the tops of the stakes to live saplings in the clearing. This meant that even heavy rain driving down could not penetrate the shelter except at the 'gable' ends where there was no cover.

'What's that whistle?' Don asked abruptly.

'Don't know,' I replied. 'Sounds like a referee blowing half-time!'

'Twelve o'clock bee,' one Indian answered with a grin.

It did sound a bit like knocking off time.

'Listen to that one, though,' said Joe. 'Sounds as if he's sawing up a log with a rusty saw.'

I think it was these weird sounding insects that most impressed us in the rain forest. It was fascinating just to listen to them. We were told of other types too; the sawyer beetle amused me particularly: this beetle attaches itself to a branch (up to one and a half inches thick) and starts to spin round it, cutting as it spins until the branch is eventually severed. The beetle usually falls with the branch, and is often found lying at the bottom of a tree together with its handiwork. But no one could tell us why they act in this manner.

The others, coming up river behind us, didn't fare so well. Alex, Gordon and Neil, who were sharing the bigger canoe with Maurice and Mike, had to take to the water on several occasions to bring the craft through the rapids. They waded through, chest deep at times, stumbling over submerged logs and branches. By the time they arrived, Neil, who was then probably the least fit of the group, was exhausted – but he had still appreciated the superb filming potential of the journey; for days after he insisted he must film the rapids sequence on the way back.

'Oh, you can get it as we go downstream,' said Don. 'The public won't know the difference.'

Neil looked at him with a puzzled frown, not knowing quite what to make of this cynical character.

The remainder of the expedition arrived in the afternoon: Adrian and Jerry occupied the last canoe, with Jonathan and a few Indians. Mike Tamessar staggered into camp on foot, complaining loudly:

'These bloody Indians! Man, I'm exhausted – they just went off and left us. I'm lucky to be here ... Ragu's behind somewhere; I may not be fit, but Ragu is a lot worse than me...'

As I hadn't yet spoken to Mike and he had seemed to be of a quiet disposition, I was rather surprised at this violent outburst so early in the expedition. It was not without reason, however, for we discovered that Ragu was really missing.

Mike continued to voice his disquiet about this fact, but neither Adrian nor Isaac seemed too worried by Ragu's absence. As Adrian said at the time, 'A child couldn't get lost up past the rapids; there's a good trail.' But good trail or not, we were missing a member and even we new boys knew the dangers of going astray in the forest. This was one thing which had really sunk home; even the Indians get lost occasionally and quite a few are never seen again. They are accustomed to spotting the thin saplings severed by the cutlass which is used for marking the trail and since most Indians are right-handed the direction of travel of the trail-maker is easy to deduce. They also break small twigs as additional markers. Ragu, however, had never been in the rain forest before and knew nothing of these things. Even if he had, it would have helped him little for we discovered – on the way out from the expedition – that our Indian guides also lost their way on this section and we could find no path or indication of previous parties.

Isaac came over to me. 'Can I borrow your torch, Mr Hamish?'

'Sure, Isaac. Here it is.' I handed him my large waterproof flashlight.

'I go look for Ragu,' he stated simply.

'Good luck, fella,' Neil said, lighting up a cigar which Joe had given to him.

The Indians communicate in the bush by a long co-oo-ee

sound, which carries well, or by beating the trunk of a tree with the handle of their cutlass. Their calls were mocked by a thousand sounds of the bush as darkness fell and fireflies, like miniature lightships, flitted aimlessly amongst the trees. None of us said much about Ragu's disappearance except Mike, who was now quieter, but each of us knew how serious the situation might be. I said to Neil; 'If he stays put for the night and doesn't panic, he should be all right.'

'Rather him than me, blue – I've no desire to have bed and breakfast in the rain forest without my gear and food; might provide breakfast for something else!'

The calls of the Indians grew faint and were eventually enveloped in the more dominant noises close at hand, noises all strange to us. About an hour later they returned and reported that there was no sign of Ragu.

'We'll get a search under way at first light,' Adrian assured us.

We slept under our mosquito nets that night and it rained heavily. It sounded as though hundreds of buckets of water were being poured from the tree tops on to our tarpaulin, or that someone had prodded the good Lord's water supply with a cutlass, directly above our camp. This didn't deter the fireflies, however.

The staccato note of an outboard motor heralded the dawn; I glanced out from under my mosquito net and saw a canoe heading downstream. A party of Indians left camp on foot at the same time to search for Ragu. The entire party was going to help search after breakfast if he hadn't been found by then. We were still eating rice and drinking tea when the canoe returned, with Ragu aboard. He staggered into camp, obviously completely shattered. Someone put a hot mug of tea into his hand.

'Thanks, maan,' he gulped it down.

He was untidier than usual, covered in mud with his long black hair plastered to his head as if he had come out of a showerbath. He had survived the night of rain unscathed and it was so warm that he had suffered little discomfort from cold.

'Man, those fuggin' Indians went off and left me,' he spat out furiously. 'Ah just stopped for about a minute to put on my other boots and they disappeared completely. Not a fuggin' sign of the skunts.'

'What did you do?' inquired Neil – making full use of this drama to get the camera going – or rather, Alex was busy with the camera whilst he plied Ragu with questions.

'I staid where I was, man, staid where I was; just found a big buttress tree and sat under it for the night. Man, I was scared.' At dawn he had heard the outboard down on the river and had staggered over to the bank where he was picked up.

'Got a good bit of film there, blue,' Neil confided to me afterwards. 'That's the stuff the public want: no namby-pamby stuff, real human interest. But what a cock-up this expedition is – have you ever been on one like it before?'

'Well,' I replied evasively. 'I've been on worse ones all right, but things don't seem to be running very smoothly. It should be okay now we're all together.'

I had noticed a tunnel which led into the forest near the small thatched cookhouse which was located at the end of the clearing. This was to be the start of our route but, as Ragu was exhausted after his benightment, Adrian decided to delay our departure until the next morning. So we spent the day drying out our personal gear – when the sun came out – and Joe even caught a few fish.

The Indians occupied this free time by making warishi baskets. These are Indian pack frames and some are beautifully executed. A simple one can be completed in a few hours, but Isaac's intricate design took almost two weeks to finish. The raw materials for making the warishi are readily available in the forest and the wicker work is bound with strips of Kakarallis bark.

As Don's foot was still bad, Adrian suggested that he should travel farther upstream in a canoe which the Indians were going to try and get through with some of the kit bags. This was arranged because there were not enough porters. Don hobbled down to the water's edge just as Joe and I set off on foot, with Alex, Gordon and Neil. They were hoping to take some film of us on the way to Camp 2.

The 1971 Expedition had found traces of the trail first made in 1928 by P. B. H. Bailey for the Geological Survey. This was the trail John Streetly, Adrian Thompson and Bev Clark had used the previous year and that we were now to follow. The path took a line parallel to the Waruma, a short distance from the river. We were walking among giants. Great buttressed trunks rose up to the canopy, over a hundred feet above our heads ; a tremendous variety for there are about four hundred common trees in these forests. The most picturesque were the stilt-rooted Maddaburi trees whose roots looked like parrot cages; the stilts can be as much as fifteen feet high, with the trunks emerging from the tops of the 'cages', and with pointed leaves arranged symmetrically in rosettes. Joe and I stopped beside yet another superb specimen; it was as if a large cluster of pipes had been fused together to make this tree of about four foot diameter, rising straight up into the foliage above like a multi-core cable.

Isaac caught us up, carrying a big load. He was up to his knees in water, fording a creek, as I shouted, 'Hey, Isaac. What kind of tree is this?' I pointed to the array of vertical columns in front of me.

He looked up, screwing his eyes, 'That's a paddle tree, Mr Hamish. We use it to make paddles and axe handles, man.'

Some of the buttress trees were extremely large, although nothing like the Sequoia gigantea which Joe and I had seen in California; but very imposing all the same, with buttress roots forming a triangular-shaped web at their base and extending twelve feet or so from the central trunk. They looked like Saturn rockets ready for take-off.

Some of the tributary streams of the Waruma – which we had to cross – were bridged by fallen trees: long, straight, and slippery, such 'bridges' are called tacoubas. Later, the Indians were using this trail almost every day while we were climbing on the face and they made handrails, supported on forked sticks, beside these bridges.

From time to time we would hear the calls of macaws from the tree tops. I caught a glimpse of a flurry of red and blue as they swept down through a partial clearing. The walking was, I thought, idyllic.

'Quite pleasant, this,' I said to Neil whom we had joined.

'This isn't jungle stuff, Hamish,' he moaned. 'It's too pretty-pretty – we could be on Loch Lomondside! The only live thing I've seen so far is Alex here, charging along like a tapir. Not a sign of a monkey or a snake.'

'I'll see what I can do,' muttered Alex.

'No doubt we'll see too many before we're finished,' I replied cheerfully. 'Someone saw a three-toed sloth from the canoe on the way up.'

'Yes, but it wasn't us,' answered Neil in disgust.

We had reached a clearing in the forest close to the river. Here the trees had been felled and the frame of an old shelter was standing like a fourlegged skeleton in the deep leafy ground. This was the site of Camp 2, but we wouldn't be using it as it wasn't far enough on for us. We were intending to travel as far as Camp 3, or even Camp 4, that day, if we were fresh enough. I put my pack down and had a breather. Seated on a fallen tree I gazed, fascinated, at the large parasol ants which were attacking the adjacent foliage. These ants cut off neat discs of green leaf and carry it in their jaws to their huge underground mushroom garden of decaying leaves.

Some of the lianas in the forest were fantastic shapes, forming great woven loops; in the denser parts of the forest there was a latticework of overhead vines, each individual vine striving to reach the canopy and obtain sunlight. The biggest lianas were over ten inches thick. I thought that some were probably Bauhinias, the source of an ingredient for curare poison. High up in the branches, there were other plants growing on the trees: epiphytes – such as bromeliads and orchids – living on the humid air, sunlight and the fragments of decaying matter which collected round their roots.

'See who can keep his feet dry longest, Joe?'

'Okay,' he responded, jumping a wide ditch. 'It'll take my mind off the lack of food.'

'Yes,' I responded. 'It's a bloody great way to start an expedition. We'll be so thin on the return trip that we'll glide through these glades like sylphs.'

But it was something to do: we were now finding the walking a bit monotonous and went to great lengths to keep dry, making long detours into the forest in search of a tacouba to avoid wading. Eventually we came to a wide area of swamp where it was obviously impossible to keep dry and we both waded through, up to our knees and laughing.

We arrived at the site of Camp 3 quite early, bursting through a curtain of bamboo to see Don and a number of Indians sitting there. Some of the porters had come ahead of us that morning and the others from the canoe were squatting round the fire.

'How do there,' said Don. 'Have a nice wee walk?'

'Aye, not bad,' I replied.

'Well, hello there,' said Joe in surprise. He was speaking to two others sitting on a log.

It was Mo and Mike. I have seldom seen two men look more bedraggled. Mo was wet and muddy, wearing a pair of horizontally striped longjohns and climbing boots. He looked tired. Mike gave the impression that he had passed through a dirty culvert which, besides depositing most of its mud on his clothing, had torn it in many places. His shirt, at one time striped and even possibly smart, now looked like limp blotting paper; an old battered bush hat completed the picture whilst several weeks' growth upon his chin made him look as if he had been in the outback all his life.

Mo told me afterwards that he was shocked at seeing how big the party had become. Like the rest of us he favoured a small compact expedition and to him the procession coming into the clearing seemed endless.

The pair of them had come back to give us a hand and lost little time in offering us a preview of the joys to come in the slime forest ahead. 'The snot hangs from the bushes, Hamish,' explained Mike with relish, 'like long drips off the nose – wonderful.' At one point they had gone off the trail and landed on a ledge on a cliff face with a 300-foot drop; it appeared the Indians didn't like the rope ladder pitch at first. Initially they refused to take their loads up it and Mo and Mike had to go down and take their warishis.

'How far did you get up?' asked Don, ever practical.

'Right up to El Dorado Swamp,' Mike said, accepting a cup of tea from one of the Indians, Maurice by name, who had been given them by Isaac. Maurice had grown on both Mike and Mo, until they had become quite attached to him. He wasn't, we were to discover, like the other Indians. He seemed to know what we wanted to learn about the jungle and showed us things, while the other porters tended to laugh if we asked them something. He was very intelligent. His shock of fine hair with a blond streak in it hung, Hitler-fashion, over his right eye from time to time. He combed it back with persistence, but remarkably little effect. He had almond-shaped eyes and was as lean and supple as a liana. Now he handed round steaming cups of tea to all of us.

Just then a diversion was created by Neil and his two stalwarts who broke into the clearing. Neil looked the part of the exhausted explorer; a mobile sweat factory, perspiration showing through his shirt and also his trousers, from the crutch down, as if he had pissed himself. 'The wet plimsoll line', as we called it.

'Hiya, guys,' he muttered, driving his five-foot anti-snake stick into the ground and lowering a large rucksack. 'Oh, how about a brew, blue?' He eyed our mugs enviously. I handed him mine, as I made the introduction to Mo and Mike.

'I thought you guys were half way up the Wall – I was getting quite worried in case you'd jumped the gun with the film.'

'No, we didn't want to be coming down from the summit as you blokes arrived at the foot of the Wall,' replied Mo smoothly.

As Joe generously shared round his personal supply of large Havanas in their metal tubes, we plied the advance party with more questions about the route and helped ourselves to pieces of mouldy 'bake'. The Indians make bake each morning whenever they have flour. It takes about an hour; a dough is made with flour and water, then fried in hot oil. The result resembles the old-fashioned scone and is also eaten cold by the Indians.

'How's the food situation up ahead?' I asked, for I had growing fears about the lack of it. We seemed to be suffering shortages already and had only been out from civilization a few days. We had been told: 'Oh, the tea and sugar is here somewhere, but we can't find it ...' – 'Tinned meat? Yes, that's in the kit bags which went up to Camp 5 three days ago,' Isaac would say, and so it went on.

'Stacks of food at Camp 6,' said Mo cheerfully – the now familiar theme – 'We took in eighteen kit bags from George-town, each containing twenty-four man-days.'

We should have had fifteen bags with us. At least that is what Joe and Don and I had packed at Adrian's farm, but we didn't know if each was for twenty-four man-days. We had tended to put in things as they came to hand, not knowing what would be needed, and there seemed to have been a hell of a lot of sweets and chocolates left over which never got packed, and whose lack we now lamented. As Don said, there seemed to have been a lot of cock-ups on this trip. To add to the general despondency, Neil was a bit worried about the film. It was so dark that Alex could hardly film anything and it was all too pretty-pretty for Neil who couldn't wait to see us up to our armpits in slime, fending off camoudis, while being bitten to death by Muniri ants. 'Those big two inch long buggers,' Neil specified with a belch, as we prepared to leave.

'O.K., test your lights, adjust your brassières and we'll go,' said Don, 'but not through any bloody swamp if I can find an alternative route!'

I was walking behind Mo. 'Your boots are in a hell of a state, Mo.'

'You're not kidding,' he replied, turning round. 'These trails are desperate. The roots are so bad between Camp 5 and 6 that we call it "root" marching. You should see the path above Camp 6. Really interesting. Mike and I have been charging around like farts in a phone booth and it's bloody dangerous too,' he continued, throwing away the stump of his cigar and balancing delicately on a long log spanning a swampy bit of ground. 'When we came up here before we were wading waist deep in water: Neil would have got all his crap and piss shots then!'

When the 1971 expedition came through this same area, they had a very wet time of it. Floods almost washed away their camps and trestles had to be built to save the equipment from being ruined. Mist nets, which they had put out to catch bats, actually contained fish the following morning!

Some wild pigs were seen by some of the party that day and two snakes were killed by the Indians, but it was mostly too wet for us to see much wild life. It wasn't very hot but we sweated profusely, mainly due to the fact that we were moving fast. We were ahead of the main party of Indians – fifteen of them – as Mo and Mike seemed to know the trail. I don't think that I would have risked travelling through that forest, relying as they did on the occasional sliced sapling as a marker, but they moved unerringly.

Though the canopy above seemed efficient at excluding light, rain poured through and we were soaked within seconds. But this didn't matter, it was warm rain: it was almost as pleasant to be wet as dry. The Indians obviously had the right idea, as they wear next to nothing in the bush, but carried a dry change with them for use in camp.

Alex and Gordon were behind us but, since we were fitter, we gradually drew ahead of them. At one stage Gordon was in front of Alex and lost the path for a short time. It was typical of the disorganization of our trip that members, with little or no forest experience, would sometimes find themselves looking in vain for the tell-tale cutlass sign of a sliced bamboo sapling, or a broken twig. When Alex and Gordon left Neil at Camp 3 they suspected that there might be some mix-up that night, so Alex asked Neil to send on their personal kit bag with their hammocks and sleeping bags. Neil sent on a rucksack, once he discovered that Isaac proposed camping at Camp 3, and the Indian carrying it did catch Alex up on the trail, but it proved to be the wrong rucksack.

'Bugger it,' – I had stumbled on a root which, like a thousand others, was looped in a snare and hidden by bamboo. I had fallen forward but, with a reflex action, had grasped a tree trunk about four inches in diameter. Long, black spikes, covering it, pierced my hand and broke off; blood poured from the wounds. This was my first encounter with the prickly palm, Astocaryum, as nasty a tree as ever grew. The spines which cover the trunk are about three-eighths of an inch long and slightly hooked to ensure that your hand – or anything else which comes into contact with them – is caught. Some of these spines are covered with moss and it is impossible to see them. We all quickly developed the Indian habit of not touching the undergrowth, or trees, if we could possibly help it. We saw one or two tarantulas, but no snakes. Everything we asked Maurice, the Indian guide, about was lethal, so I carefully avoided seeking his opinion of the prickly palm. But my hand was certainly sore.

Mo, for his part, thought that some of the juice from one of the trees up above had burnt his hand slightly, and I remembered reading about certain sap causing blisters.

It was about 3 p.m. when we arrived in the clearing beside the river which contained Camp 4. It had taken us four hours, walking, from Camp 1. Admittedly, it wasn't a normal four hour walk – more like an obstacle course for budding Tarzans. The camps were set up so close together because they were originally intended as working bases for the early geological survey party.

The forest was still riverain in nature, but about Camp 4 there were bamboos and small palms and I noticed that tentacles of moss hung down from the tree branches. Had anyone witnessed our arrival, they would have seen our packs dropped unceremoniously on the ground as, almost without breaking step, we jumped straight into the river with all our clothes on. All that could be seen of Joe was a hat and a large cigar above the surface; he looked more like a smoke float than a human being.

'What about all the perai and caimen?' I shouted.

'Fuck them,' said Mo. 'They'll have plenty of salt to go with their meal, at any rate.'

'I can see Roraima from here,' said Don, washing his clothes by rubbing them against his skin with his hands, for he was fastidious about this. 'Good view of it.' It must have been about seven miles away, but we could see the Prow quite clearly.

'Not taking any film?' I asked Alex in surprise.

'Oh, the usual has happened; when I can get some decent stuff, the film is with a porter who has vanished. Dear knows where he is. Oh yes,' he added, 'he also has Fred, with all our personal things. Lesson number 50: never be separated from your personal gear in the jungle!' (The kit bags were ex-W.D. and were stencilled with the names of their original owners, but the film crew's had been rechristened Fred in Georgetown when Alex had a marker pen to hand.) Alex felt sick, I discovered and had bad cramp in both thighs, so I suggested he take a spoonful of salt.

I had a look in the bed of the river for diamonds, but didn't see anything except odd bits of pyrites. Isaac told me his brother-in-law had some reasonable luck further down.

'Have you lost your halfpence – that coin you keep on a bit of elastic for tipping waiters?' asked Don.

'Ha, ha, Whillans,' I muttered disgustedly.

In the river there was plenty of Pakuweed, so called by the Indians because the Paku fish is supposed to feed on it, but there were no fish up here; Joe later confirmed this after a few futile casts. This seaweed-like plant clings with sucker-type organs to rocks and they offer little resistance to the fast-flowing water. They can live submerged for very long periods. During the dry season, as the water level drops, and they are exposed to the air, the stalks and roots begin to decay; the flower buds then swell open and sets seed very rapidly (within the space of a few days), obviously geared to complete the cycle before the next flood.

I was first out of the river – dripping wet, but my clothes looked considerably cleaner. I started to sling my hammock from the frame of the shelter, near the middle, away from any driving rain which tends to penetrate via the ends. The others joined me and followed suit.

'You look a bit dejected sitting there, Gordon,' said Don, tying a bowline on his hammock line. 'Why don't you get organized for the night?'

'We would like to, I assure you,' answered Gordon in his precise way. 'But, unfortunately,' he waved his hand pointedly, 'as our valet has mislaid Fred we shall, I presume, remain seated on this log, watching the steady encroachment of ants and vampires. We have no mosquito nets, not even a sleeping bag between us!'

'Aye, one learns fast on these trips,' remarked Don sagely.

Alex confided to me that he felt weak through lack of food. He had had little to eat for several days now and some of the porters back at Camp 3 hadn't eaten for three days.

Maurice produced a yellow tarpaulin, however, and another porter who had come with him had brought food; a fire was going in the small thatched hut which was presumably erected on the 1971 expedition. Maurice gave us some hot water and powdered milk. We helped ourselves to sugar after fighting our way down through a colony of stingless bees (one of the few stingless creatures in this forest, I thought to myself).

'Hey, Maurice, do you carry these bees from camp to camp in this jar?' I asked.

'No, su,' replied Maurice. 'There are plenty in each camp.' His expression was deadpan.

Dusk was falling before we realized that the others would not be coming that night. We found out later that Isaac had planned for us all to stay at an intermediate clearing that night, somewhere between Camps 3 and 4, and was very annoyed to find we had continued. Don, for one, had felt like moving on, away from the large group, for he likes to travel with the minimum of fuss when he is on the march; I must say that I sympathized with him in this respect. But it caused some ill-feeling and obviously didn't help relations between the climbers and the remainder of the group, which already seemed to be two separate entities.

It was obvious that Alex and Gordon were going to have a hard night. Alex inspected a trestle with deep suspicion; a barbricot table made from long thin branches with saplings at the four corners which served as somewhat delicate legs. It was bound together with strips of bark from the monkey pipe tree. Six feet long and eighteen inches wide, it was well that Alex's frame was less than normal in stature.

'I don't think it's quite up to Highland Hotel standard,

Gordon,' Alex observed, testing it for spring. 'But I suppose we'll both have to squeeze on to it.'

I donated them a pullover and an anorak, and Don handed over his orange parka. The sandflies and the mosquitoes were our main trouble, here and at Camp 5.

'Things like Concordes flying about, and other bastards like dodgem-cars,' said Mo, drawing on a fag. 'None of the Indians like staying at 5, it's on a swamp.'

Neil had remained with the main party and later told me that one of the reasons Isaac had wished to have a shorter day from Camp 1 was that he didn't have enough porters. This trouble, together with the lack of food, resulted in a total stoppage while Neil had spent some time pleading with the Indians to try and get them organized for the following day. Adrian had no success either, and we never really got to the bottom of the trouble, or discovered how it was finally sorted out. Isaac was never very forthcoming on the subject. Neil told me that the Indians had threatened to pack up and go home:

'And their packing wouldn't have taken them long, blue!' he added vehemently. 'Their dry change into their warishis, and they're off...'

We were all lying idly in our hammocks. There was always a tense moment as the last man got in, for the shelter frame was continually expected to collapse, but seldom actually did. While we were lying there, talking about our favourite meals (always an overworked topic when food is short), Mo grasped Joe's hammock and started to swing it. There is something peaceful about swinging in a hammock; I suppose it goes back to our non-existent cradle days, or something similar. We had already observed that the Indians could start swinging without pushing on anything – probably the same sort of action as a kid uses on a swing. Joe started to push Mo more violently and himself hit Don – who was on his other side – on his counter swing. Don then grasped my hammock, like Tennyson's eagle, and a chain reaction was set up with six hammocks, like crazy airborne canoes, threatening to loop the loop. The shelter heaved and groaned but fortunately withstood the onslaught.

Alex and Gordon obviously had a terrible night; I could hear the constant drone of mosquitoes and sandflies from inside my net. The two stalwarts were sleeping at right-angles to our hammocks, directly under one of the main longitudinal supports of the shelter. As a matter of fact, had either of them been possessed of a long nose, it would have fouled the slender saplings which served as our joint hammock anchor. The deck of their barbricot table was only inches away from it. In the morning their faces were pockmarked with bites.

Though Don and the others were keen to carry on ahead of the main party, it was obviously impossible unless we could get food and dixies. We had virtually nothing left to eat, so I volunteered to await the other group, get some food and cooking gear from them; then travel up to Camp 5 that afternoon with Oswald, a fast-moving Indian who had been up to Camp 7 with Mo and Mike. This was agreed upon but Alex and Gordon decided they should await their equipment, as well as their delayed Director.

Don and Joe departed after a token breakfast of hot milk, as the rain of the first-light had diminished to a mere dribble.

'I'm glad the tap's turned off,' remarked Gordon, looking up. 'Could do with getting some washing dry.'

'I'm going to have mine done in Georgetown when I get back,' I said grandly. 'But that'll be the gear I return in.' I had enough spare clothes with me to throw them away as they got dirty, but as Gordon and Alex were visualizing four or five porters carying my wardrobe, I explained that this amounted to just two sets of underclothes and three pairs of socks.

'Well, I suppose that makes life fairly simple,' observed Gordon, hanging out his newly laundered shirt. 'We've started a dirty underpants competition – but only between

Neil, Alex and myself. Climbers are not allowed to compete.'

'Don couldn't enter anyway,' I replied, casually crushing a large poisonous centipede. 'He doesn't wear them ... Anyhow,' I continued, 'whoever in your group comes up the Prow a bit with us is sure to win hands down!'

Neil came into camp, his white staff – a stick with freshly peeled bark – allying him to John the Baptist, or the front pages of *Scouting for Boys*.

'Hiya, blue,' he greeted me. 'Hello, fellahs,' he said to his two colleagues as he sat down on his rucksack. 'What a bloody mess! Do you know, we've had a ruddy strike on our hands back there,' he jerked his thumb backwards in the direction he had just come. 'If you ask me, it's a case of too many chiefs and not enough Indians ... Where are the others?' he looked around anxiously.

'Gone up to 5,' I said. 'I'll join them when I've collected some food.'

'Jesus Christ, what about the fucking film?' he shouted, throwing down his stick. 'How the hell can we film if you buggers are up ahead and we're a camp behind?'

'Can't you all come along with us?' I suggested hopefully.

'Look, blue,' said Neil, wiping his sweaty brow with the back of his hand. 'I can't even get a couple of Indians to carry the ruddy film gear, and that was definitely promised – I made a particular point with Adrian that it was absolutely imperative. But he's not got enough porters. I've never seen such a goddamn badly organized trip in my life.'

We pacified Neil by pointing out that it was too dark for filming so far anyway and that we'd promise to be co-operative at Camp 6 and give him all the trail shots he wanted. Mo had told us the scenery was fantastic up there and if it was also to be the base camp for the main part of the expedition, at least things would get better organized there in time. We hoped.

The rain started again with a vengeance. It was as if each

deluge was in direct competition with the last, in an endless quest to create a new record. When it finally eased, I suggested to Oswald that we had better get going if we were to reach Camp 5 before dark.

'We must go fast,' he replied, picking up his warishi. He was dressed only in a pair of shorts. Another Indian was coming with us as well, bringing a tarpaulin.

'See you, chaps,' I called as I set off at a jog-trot after my intrepid Indian guide, weaving our way through the endless slalom of the forest. After about two hundred yards we had to wait for the other Indian to catch up. Oswald shouted to him in his native tongue, something scathing, I presume, and the Indian moved as if injected with a bumper dose of adrenalin.

Moving fast through the forest was like looking through a kaleidoscope with unbelievable shades of green. Occasionally we saw vivid blood-red pools (there are no streams on this section of the trail) as a stray shaft of light caught the water for a breathtaking moment. As I raced along in the footsteps of Oswald, I wondered how many snakes and spiders we frightened away as we broke through the undergrowth, but I didn't see any. It was a montane forest, with a profusion of ferns and Selaginella.

We arrived at Camp 5 in the late afternoon. First impression of the place was unpleasant, but when one took a look about it was more than that: it was nasty. Evil, boggy ground and humidity at saturation point obviously contributed to this atmosphere, but there was something intangible besides, which I couldn't put my finger on. I knew instantly why the Indians disliked the camp.

'Ah, it's the wandering Scotsman himsel'. Who are you doing, Jock?'

'It certainly won't be you buggers, anyhow,' I retorted. 'You're all too cunning and twisted as the vines.'

'Have you any grub?' asked Joe practically.

'Yes, and a spare tarpaulin.'

'Bit of Dundee fruit cake there for you, lad,' offered Mo. 'Great stuff.'

'Thanks,' I took it gratefully as I slung my hammock. We had already learnt not to sit down on logs and always, without fail, to shake out our boots before putting them on. One is quick to pick up the tips necessary to more comfortable living in the jungle.

We all slept reasonably well that night, though it rained incessantly. As I looked out from under the shelter (inevitably, having arrived late, I was demoted to the 'gable'-end), the vista was one of disenchantment: trees dripped with water and long fingers of moss hung like tinkers' washing from branches. Other trees, having lost the support of those which had at one time occupied the clearing, were listing dangerously, giving the place the appearance of bomb-shelled territory or as if devastated by an airborne avalanche. The camp was astir and the Indians had a fire going. I was interested in their methods of lighting a fire under these inauspicious conditions of almost constant saturation.

'Well, su,' Maurice enlightened me. 'We get the bark of this tree,' he pointed to a large tree with a stringy bark, 'And we use it with very fine bits of wood, and we build this up to let plenty of air in. Then we pour paraffin over it!'

So much for my brain-washing when I was a boy scout, I thought cynically.

Mo and Joe set off first, followed by most of the Indians and Mike. Maurice, Don and I took up the rear. As Mo had predicted, this was real 'root' marching. Snake rooted cork-woods and prickly palm were there in abundance. It was as if we were walking on a morass of cables in a TV studio, all colours and shapes. The 'cages' of the stiltrooted Maddaburi (Clusia) trees looked sinister – probably the homes of lethal insects, I thought morbidly. I visualized myself imprisoned in one, being eaten alive by soldier ants.

'You know, Don,' I said as I stopped to take a photograph

of a large Caligo butterfly. 'Some of the bamboo found further south is poisonous.' Down on the Rappu river, a tributary of the Essequebo, the Indians use it for arrowheads. It's supposed to have a poison similar to Wourali or Curare.

'Hey, Hamish,' Don said, looking through the viewfinder of his waterproof camera. 'Stand beside that tree whilst I take a picture,' – he either wasn't listening or he didn't care.

Don always sets a somewhat leisurely preamble, making for his various objectives, be they the local pub or Mount Everest. The pace was further reduced that day because his foot was still troubling him. I didn't mind at all as I'd had enough rushing the previous day and had bruised my instep on a root. In fact, my foot had penetrated a leaf-covered hole to encounter a further broken end at the bottom of it – like a native pit trap, furnished with a pointed stake for catching and killing wild animals. There were thousands of these 'pot-holes' and an ample supply of leaves, which were about two feet long, to camouflage them. This 'slow march' was obviously more than Maurice could stand; like a dog keen to go for a long-promised walk, he would forge ahead and then look back at us, as if willing us to move faster.

It was an idyllic day – the rain only equivalent to a heavy deluge in Britain at times – and when we came to the edge of a swift-flowing river, cascading down a sandstone boulder-strewn bed, we decided to stop.

'Fancy a sit by the river, lad?'

'Ay, good idea,' I agreed. 'I've a Dundee cake with me.'

'Oh, we've got to look after number one,' said Don with enthusiasm.

I started prospecting, washing the gravel in the cake tin as soon as we had disposed of its contents. There were a few interesting concentrates, but no gold.

As soon as we started moving again, the sweat taps turned on, but the sweat was soon diluted as, once again, the heavens opened. We were following the river's course. The moss-covered trees were like vertical cylindrical sponges; when we touched them accidentally, the water would run up our arms.

'Spider, Mr Don!'

Maurice, who was just ahead of Don, pointed to a large hairy Theraphosa, the bird-eating spider which can jump several feet, and when I urged him to catch it for me he equipped himself with two sticks and pinioned the creature with them whilst I conjured up a plastic bag from my pocket; I was already envious of Joe's 'Henry', a large weird-looking flying insect he had caught, which looked remarkably like a combine harvester at work, and I wanted to better this trophy, though my spider was only a mere infant of seven inches across and I'd heard they go up to about twelve inches. The poor beast was eventually incarcerated and with Maurice holding the bag nonchalantly by its neck, we continued on our way.

The trail started to rise noticeably. We had been climbing since leaving Camp 1, of course, but it had been almost imperceptible until now. The undergrowth was getting more dense as well. There was much more in evidence amongst the big trees and trail making would have been very hard work.

'No chance of losing one's way now,' commented Don.

'No, it's like walking in a trench,' I agreed, brushing a sinewy vine from my face.

We crossed a small stream and there ahead of us, beyond some large fallen trees lay Camp 6 and Mike to greet us with a brew up and some 'snake and pygmy' pudding to follow. Everyone gathered round to admire my spider. He was certainly one better than Henry. Joe, who had an avid interest in the insect kingdom, was soon offering Maurice four dollars for a bigger one, and six for a Hercules beetle.

I left Joe to his reckless extravagance and took stock of Camp 6. It was pleasantly cooler. A large shelter – about forty feet long – had been built in two separate sections. Our three friends had already organized their hammocks, hanging there limply between the frame members, and were unpacking their gear. A small shelter constructed from saplings and thatched with palm leaves served as the cookhouse. Two of the Indians were applying the mouth to mouth technique to the fire which was in danger of dying – no doubt they had run out of paraffin!

'Joe killed a snake on the way up today,' Mo told us.

'Big one?' I asked.

'No, a tiddler,' replied Joe honestly.

'Good God, look at that!' I exclaimed, dropping the end of my hammock and running outside the shelter. 'What a sight!'

The Prow of Roraima had come partially into view: a great red lump of monolithic rock, rising like a tombstone from the green ridge above us, and wreathed with tree ferns and epiphytes. It was breathtaking. The others rushed out from under the tarpaulin as though it were the wrath of Samson descending upon the Philistines.

'Hey, what's the exposure, Hamish?' Don demanded, gazing upwards.

'A hundred at f.11.'

'Blimey, it looks fantastic,' Joe was ecstatic.

It was certainly a fine bit of rock. I grabbed a pair of binoculars; too late, it vanished, veiled once again by cloud, making me think of the old Indian belief that Roraima could never be seen cloud-free by a white man.

We were eating our steak and kidney pudding and rice after our dramatic viewing of Roraima when Adrian burst into camp. He had come all the way from Camp 3 that day but looked as fresh as ever, even his green shirt still had a crease in the sleeves. He was accompanied by Isaac Jerry and a couple of Indians. The others, including the BBC group were spending the night at Camp 5. Alex noted in his diary that day: 'Tree Root Camp, Camp 5 ... I was weak with hunger and had my usual shaking. We really have to get more to eat; one meal of rice a day is not enough.'

Isaac set to work, with the two Indians, to build another

shelter; in about an hour a large structure was completed. The men worked with a quiet efficiency which was a joy to watch. The completed frame was a superb example of structural engineering, designed to hold about ten people suspended from the two long parallel frame members.

The helicopter, with all our personal climbing gear on board, was not due in for three days, so Mike and Mo decided to go on next day to establish Camp 7, taking Maurice and a couple of porters. We spent part of the evening sorting out the kit bags and haul bags which they had brought up with them. The pile seemed pathetically small, I thought, comparing it to the huge caches of gear needed on high altitude trips. We unearthed a couple of big Gaz stoves for the Indians, who were still blowing their reluctant fire within the open shelter of the cookhouse, which was simply a structure with an angled, thatched roof, like a lean-to with nothing to lean on except its integral poles, arranged goalpost fashion.

I had already mentioned to Adrian my misgivings – which Don shared – about the quantity of food available. I brought the subject up again as he unpacked his rucksack under the newly-roofed shelter. A brand new yellow p.v.c tarpaulin was stretched neatly over it.

'About the food, Adrian,' I began tentatively. 'I feel there isn't nearly enough.'

'Oh, plenty of food, Hamish,' he smiled and waved his hand in a carefree gesture as though magically offering a cornucopia. 'Mo and Mike packed it all.'

'Well, I can't see it,' I reiterated stubbornly. 'I've seen the kit bags here, and by the looks of things, we've only enough for a few more days.'

'Oh, that's impossible,' he replied. 'We had plenty of food.'

Adrian has a most endearing way with him and I didn't want to offend him further at that moment, just after his long hard walk from Camp 3; though I was determined to bring the matter up the following day. Adrian is one of the fittest men, for his age, that I have ever met. In earlier days he was able to keep pace with, and even travel farther than, most of the indigenous Indians – moving with unerring celerity through difficult forest terrain. He gives the impression of being taller than he actually is – probably because he holds himself so erect – but is in fact about six foot. He brought some fine orchids into camp with him; he told me afterwards that a very rare plant could cost as much as £500.

'You know, Joe,' I remarked later as I took off my boots – sugar cane worker's boots which had been presented to us in Georgetown by the Bata company – 'This place reminds me of a building site; the mud must be ten inches deep in places.'

'More like a drainage site,' corrected Joe, better versed than I in building technicalities. A stream ran alongside the Camp and, despite the quagmire, it was in fact by far the best stopping place we had found to date.

At this latitude the sun never wanders far from the Equator and there is little variation in daylight hours at any time of the year. In the forest (jungle is a nasty word and not normally used in Guyana as it suggests a tangled mass of thorns and lianas!), we had already fallen into the habit of going to bed as it grew dark – about 6.30 p.m. – and getting up at first-light – 6 a.m. On a trip such as this one got quite a few hammock hours in altogether. Adrian, knowing the importance of hammocks, had bought Indian ones for the expedition; they were elegantly tassled and, though they were on the heavy side, were remarkably comfortable. The Amerindians spend all their leisure hours in them, lying diagonally, as they are extremely broad.

By now we were all hypersensitive about the possibility of being stung or bitten, and kept our snake sticks handy. Mine was an adapted terrordactyl – the specialized climbing tool I used to manufacture for ascending vertical ice. The addition of an old stretcher shaft had turned it into an excellent walking stick. Round the fire that night I confessed to a terrifying false alarm the previous day. I had been going along the track when I trod on a stick almost totally covered by fallen leaves. It was about four feet long and the far end reared up when I trod on it. In a purely reflex action (no doubt keyed up by anti-snake propaganda) I whacked it with the 'terror', thinking it was a bushmaster, or something equally virulent. I could laugh about it now, but we all noticed that Adrian, the most experienced of us, never went into the forest without his stick and his small survival bag.

Chapter 7

... 'He had not wholly quenched his power;
  A little grain of conscience made him sour,'
At last I heard a voice upon the slope
Cry to the summit, 'Is there any hope?'

'The Vision of Sun', *Tennyson*

'How the hell a nation could inflict this bloody stuff on the rest of the world is beyond my comprehension,' muttered Don in disgust. 'Just imagine, at the base of the Lost World and we still get it!' It was the second morning we had submitted to thick, lumpy porridge for breakfast and I was finding it increasingly difficult to defend our national dish.

'Have you any plastic bags, Hamish?' asked Joe.

'I can give you one,' I said, handing him a large black one. Though we didn't realize it at the time, this was the beginning of what Alex called 'the plastic bag syndrome'. We had packed over 500 bags in all shapes and sizes, but they always seemed to be in short supply; later in the expedition, we coveted them as though they were chocolate biscuits.

'I think we'll hit the trail,' said Mo. He and Mike had already packed huge rucksacks. As they put them on, they towered high above their heads. The Indians accompanying them were similarly loaded. Mike was wearing his well-worn shorts; Mo, his striped longjohns. With a brief 'Be seeing ya', they were off, up the steep bank that formed the uphill side of the clearing behind Adrian's doss, and in an instant they were swallowed up by the forest.

Camp 6 was a phenomenal breeding ground for plant life. The epiphytic plants were possibly the most striking; growing, as they did, in the most unlikely places. One great buttress tree, in particular, was the host for countless vines and plants. Indeed, it was difficult to distinguish it, for it was draped, like a coat hanger, with a mantle of greenery. Great lianas festooned the upper branches, forming a gently waving curtain, while humming birds hovered ecstatically, their wings whirring like electric fan blades in a blur of light.

It was a good day; the sun came out and directed a stream of heat down into the clearing like a blowlamp, the sort of intensity which is only found close to the Equator. We hung our damp clothes out to dry on a long horizontal sapling and washed in the bubbling stream, which leapt down through the boulders littering the forest floor.

I spent the morning writing up the *Observer* report on some pages out of Joe's triplicate invoicing book. This is Joe's method of letter-home-writing – a copy each for his wife and his daughter and one for himself, and he goes back with a notebook a third of the size he started out with. Don washed and sorted out some more climbing gear. Joe's Henry and my spider hung peacefully in their respective polythene bags at the end of the shelter. Looking upwards, I could see the cloud swirling round the base of the Prow; almost as if performing the dance of the veils, it afforded tantalizing glimpses of the red rock.

Presently I heard a shout. I dropped my notes and swung out of my hammock to see Neil, looking dishevelled and exhausted; his crumpled blue bush hat pulled down over his head, his shirt unbuttoned and gaping like swing doors of a bar. Already, his stomach was diminishing (he examined it minutely each day and would seek our opinion anxiously).

' "But who are ye in rags and rotten shoes",' (I quoted glibly from Flecker). ' "You dirty-bearded, blocking up the way?"'

' "We are the Pilgrims, Master;"' (he replied promptly, raising his stick).

> '. . . we shall go
> Always a little further: it may be
> Beyond that last blue mountain . . .'

'I didn't know you knew "Hassan",' I said in surprise.

'I didn't know you knew "Hassan", blue! We must quote to each other sometime.'

Don came out from under the shelter.

'Hiya,' he called. 'If it's no the Mad Crapper himself.'

'You know, Don, I'm buggered, absolutely buggered. That was one of the worst walks of my life,' Neil said with feeling.

Alex and Gordon arrived shortly afterwards, Alex clutching his Eclair as usual, followed by most of the others, though not Ragu or Mike who were still grinding up the final slope in bottom gear. Alex wasn't looking at all well and I was concerned about him, though Gordon seemed in reasonable fettle. That morning they had only had three spoonfuls of mashed potato and three water biscuits for breakfast. The lack of food was telling on them.

Throughout the remainder of the day expedition members trudged wearily into camp. Both Ragu and Mike were extremely tired. As Ragu said, 'Good God, man, I never thought I could have done that . . . I thought I was going to die, man.'

Indeed, he didn't look too well either. Sweat poured from his body and his trousers and shirt were ripped. He subsided on to some kit bags, rather like a deflating balloon. The camp was now a hive of industry; some tea was quickly produced for the latest arrivals.

I happened to notice that Neil had carefully deposited a plastic bag on his rucksack.

'What's in the conservatory?' I inquired.

'Oh, it's just a bird-eating spider I caught – evil looking chap, isn't he?'

'I've got one, too,' I pointed to where my livestock was suspended by the bootlace which secured the neck of the polythene bag. 'He can share my bootlace – there's enough there to tie up yours too.'

'We saw several others as well,' Gordon commented. 'But we didn't catch them.'

These large Theraphosa spiders seemed to be common only at the altitude of Camp 6, which is about 4,000 feet. According to Isaac, they are smaller both below and above.

I had done another check on the food and worked out that on our present starvation rations we had enough for seven more days. We had just finished all the existing tea and sugar. So what, I asked Adrian, had happened to the rest of that for a start? But Adrian was still vague about the situation. Don, on the other hand, was not, and he was in one of his determined moods. I knew the warning signs well; Adrian didn't. By the time Don had finished telling him what he thought of his organization and method Adrian was visibly shaken. Nevertheless, when Isaac Jerry was questioned about the missing supplies, he could only suggest the food was in the kit bags left down at Camp 3 which should arrive the next day.

'The sooner we get up on that face from this circus, the better,' said Don in disgust, his outburst subsiding. 'And we won't want the whole ruddy menagerie up at Camp 7, either. Mo says there's no room up there, for a kick-off,' he stalked back to our shelter with a final outraged volley: 'Spies, BBC, and flower-pickers ... We came here to climb that thing up there,' he pointed with his Swiss Army knife emphatically in the direction of the Prow.

I had scarcely time to reach our shelter before the next crisis arose. Our Indians were quitting partly because the pay wasn't enough, partly because they'd been asked to work on Saturday and were Seventh Day Adventists.

We all realized how serious this was; we were already short of porters and these were all strong and willing. Neil did a film interview with them before they left: they were quite happy to admit that they didn't like this rain forest and could earn as much in their native villages, although they were getting the recommended pay, as decreed by the Government, with the deduction of the legal health contribution.

That evening it rained as if it was trying to make up for a

hundred years of drought. Droplets, the size of peanuts, bounced a good eighteen inches off the deep layer of mud, so great was the force of the deluge I was snug in my hammock, as was everyone except Neil, watching this torrential downpour. When Neil, with an agility belying his forty-four years, swung himself on board there was an almighty crash as one of the main supports gave way and half a dozen helpless bodies crashed to the ground. I then realized that the redeeming feature of the gable-end hammock is only evident in moments of crisis: being closest to the main uprights, it is not so likely to cause an undignified fall in the mud. As it turned out, I only suffered a jolt which was quite adequately absorbed by the resilience of my hammock, although my subsequent laughter almost caused me to capsize, nevertheless! As assorted minimally clothed bodies picked themselves swearing out of the mud, I felt moved to continue my selected quotations from the New Testament for their improvement: 'And the rain descended and the floods came, and the winds blew, and beat upon that house; and it fell: and great was the fall of it. Matthew seven verse twenty-seven,' I said.

'You're a jammy bugger, MacInnes, just look at my hammock. Covered in muck,' grieved Joe.

Sunday 14 October was treated as an off day by everyone. Ragu had acquired a new lease of life after his gruelling walk the previous day, and went off cheerfully into the forest with an Indian and a fistful of plastic bags.

'There's some nice stuff up here, man,' he beamed as he lurched enthusiastically out of camp like a plump camel, forgetting his stiffness in his eagerness.

'I think I'll move up to Camp 7,' Don peered up to the sky through a green tunnel. 'Doesn't look too bad. Can't stand all these blighters farting about like blue-arsed flies. There're too many plans flying around; it's like crapping on a fan blade.'

In a matter of minutes he was packed and, as Mo would

need more food, we quickly made up a couple of 40-lb. loads for two porters who would return to Camp 6 after their carry. Don set off hard on the heels of the porters, carrying his red frame rucksack and wearing Joe's blue cap which he had nefariously acquired.

Jonathan photographed plants and flowers for Adrian. One tiny orchid had leaves scarcely 3 mm. in width. Maurice the Spy dashed about with his Bolex, emulating Alex and obviously enjoying himself, but neither he nor Jonathan endeared themselves to the rest of us. There was evidently some rivalry between them and each was inclined to make scathing remarks about the other. Their fathers both held responsible positions in Guyana; Maurice's father was a Cabinet Minister and Jonathan's an executive in Bookers.

There was never an off day for Alex. At all times of the day, Neil would come up and ask for a filming sequence. Now, Alex's answer was brief and to the point:

'No film, Neil.'

'Jesus Christ, I forgot,' said Neil. 'It was too dark down below and now, when we have the opportunity to film, we don't have the bloody film.'

'We could take a short sequence showing the spiders,' suggested Alex. 'Have them parading along a log, or something? It wouldn't take much film.'

'Okay, let's do that. At least we'll have something in the can.'

As guinea pig, my hand was resting on the shelter frame; I was supposed to be looking up towards the Prow, which cleared intermittently, whilst a large bird-eating spider, crawling along the trunk, approached my hand. I very nearly brought off the impossible feat of operating one eye at right-angles to the other, as I knew, from past experience with dedicated film makers, that they would be unlikely to tell me when the spider had reached the agreed one inch from my fingers! Admittedly, Adrian seemed unconcerned about these spiders and even allowed them to walk over the backs of his hands. I asked one of the Indians if the bite had ever been known to kill anyone; he replied that he thought not, unless one happened to be weak at the time, but you might be very ill for several days. Scorpions were more dangerous, I learnt, and more plentiful.

Morning routine: sounds of the Indians, vainly trying to blow up a fire from splinters of wet sticks. They had almost run out of paraffin and there was only enough left for Adrian's lantern, a device, I learnt later, which would keep vampire bats at bay (not that there were many in this region, despite our former panic). Listening to the rain lashing down, Gordon took some recordings but when he played them back it made such a racket that he decided he probably couldn't use it: People, he said, would never believe rain could make a noise like the Glasgow Police Pipe Band drummers, starting with an eight stroke roll and continuing with an ear-splitting tattoo. After such refreshing thoughts, if it was imperative, I used my piss-tin, conveniently placed at arm's reach on the mud (we were loath to leave the sanctuary of the hammock after dark, especially with no boots on). Then I would draw the mosquito net aside carefully, for this was a special and delicate mini-mesh mosquito net (a select item from Bookers Stores, Georgetown), and peer outside into the green hell. One advantage of being a gable-end sleeper was that you had all the joy of the early morning view of the rain forest: dripping and slimy like the fur of a drowned rabbit.

If there was a chance of anything better than porridge for breakfast, I would struggle into my pyjamas, whilst next door Joe would bring up a horrible green snot with chest-wracking retching; because he knew it disgusted me, he would deposit it between our hammocks where he knew there was a fair chance that I would tread during the course of the day.

Neil, just two hammocks away, would have ceased his snoring by now; the note was only a few decibels lower than that of the fifty h.p. Evinrude outboard of the Guyana Defence Force. It would stop as abruptly as it began, as if the ignition had been cut. Neil reminded me of an engine, or perhaps a generator, in many ways. He would hum with activity all day; charging here, there, and everywhere like a positive electron, always dabbling and doing small jobs which the Indians were paid to do and could do much quicker.

Such odd streams of thought used to run through my mind during those early morning interludes as the world began to stir. My boots would be alongside my hammock (on the opposite side from Brown) and I would reach down to shake each in turn, like an intrepid explorer, then lower my feet into them and stand up, whereupon the boots would sink yet another inch into the ground, for the layer of mud grew deeper and softer every day.

'I'll have "conny" (condensed milk) in my gravel today please, Oswald,' I said that morning. 'And only one or two stingless bees, if they still taste of honey.'

'Right, Mr Hamish, coming up shortly. Fire not good today.'

'Not good any day,' I muttered. 'You need Baden-Powell here for a week or so to give you a few lessons.'

'Who is he?' asked the talkative Oswald (he was the short, broad-faced sturdy Indian who had gone up to Camp 5 with me).

'Oh, he was a bugger who could make a fire under the Kaieteur Falls ... But there was another man called Prometheus who was better; he first stole fire from the missionaries and they were really annoyed about it. They had him chained to a big rock like Roraima and he stayed there for 30,000 years, with Harpi eagles eating his liver. In the end he was freed by a strong man – like Mr Don.'

'Don't you believe a word of it,' Neil warned as he came over with his dixy lid for his morning fare. 'He's just trying to get more porridge from you.'

'Zero Delta, Zero Delta,' Cham sent out his latest progress report and an urgent message from Neil, requiring information about the helicopter lift, since the BBC crew were almost out of film. We had finished breakfast – all two spoonfuls of porridge – when Cham came over to Adrian with the message that they were 'having some trouble' with the helicopter. Neil gritted his teeth but said nothing. I don't think he dared open his mouth at that moment; he would have exploded in fury. We sat down in the shelters and watched the rain which beat down relentlessly until the ground was awash and the gentle stream, which we had admired on our arrival, became a raging torrent.

It was at 4 o'clock that the news – not entirely unexpected to me – came through: the helicopter had broken down and they had no idea when spares would be available.

I think it was at that instant we all realized the seriousness of the situation. A few simple words spelled out possible disaster to our expedition, which Adrian had dreamt about for a score of years and to which we had all contributed our various skills. The rain, the mud, and the general depression which had been building up over the last few days, seemed now to be concentrated on that scrap of notepaper on which Cham had written down the message. Neil raised both arms – the gesture of a drowning man going down for the third time – and didn't say a word. Our El Dorado was crumbling fast. Adrian went silently back to his shelter and sat down on the first-aid box.

I was standing in the cookhouse lean-to, trying to avoid the smoke from the campfire (which is never seen in movie films). The usual cacophony of whistles and squeaks could be heard in the forest. The peak above was still busy manufacturing cloud like a candy floss machine and arrows of rain now slanted down from the north-west.

Adrian called me over. I stooped under the tarpaulin and sat on Isaac's hammock.

'Hamish,' he began. 'I think we must discuss tactics. I know the food situation is acute and I know that filming has almost come to a halt through lack of stock. There is only one thing to do: Isaac and I, together with a few Indians, must return to Maiurapai and collect the food, film and climbing gear. Isaac will have to go round the villages and try to recruit more Indians.'

'But it's a hell of a trip to Maiurapai,' I objected. Adrian seemed more composed now, but my mind boggled at the thought of him, at the age of sixty-one, undertaking the two-way trip to the Kako river. 'It could take ages.'

'No, Hamish, I've just discussed it with Isaac. If we cut across to the trail up the Paikwa river which John Streetly, Isaac and I cut last April, we could be back within a week. And I'll order food by radio from Georgetown this afternoon. My brother will buy it as soon as I get a message to him. Bob Fernandez can go into Georgetown and collect it.'

'That forest across to the Paikwa is unexplored, isn't it?'

'Oh yes,' he replied. 'But I'm sure that we'll make it all right. You see, I think that it will be a much faster route. When John and I came over in April, we tried to cut across to Roraima from too far up the Paikwa, but the lower trail we made was good.'

Adrian was obviously under a lot of pressure. He generally acts as the Eric Shipton of Guyana, taking small compact expeditions into the interior where, to a great extent, they can rely on food from the native villages; at least, he had only to deal with the needs of a few expert bushmen. This large cumbersome centipede of an expedition he was now involved with had more than doubled in size since he first thought of returning to the Prow. It had been too much to ask of him; he had had first of all to unravel all the official red tape before he left Georgetown, working long hours and achieving miraculous results through his contacts with the

Government; and we were probably as much to blame as anyone for the resultant chaos.

About half an hour afterwards the high voice of Maurice 'the Spy' piped up from near my end of the shelter:

'Whose spider is this on the support, man? It's escaped from its plastic bag!'

We were out of our hammocks in an instant, where we had been occupied, either reading or adjusting our cameras and gear.

We descended *en masse* to where my spider was stalking furiously along the main hammock support under the tarpaulin. No one seemed very keen on recapturing it. I suppose that I'd have been angry too, if I'd been tied in a transparent bivouac sack for a couple of days with nothing to eat. Old Hairy reared up on his four hind legs, displaying a set of fangs, like a hasp staple. He was eventually returned to the bag by Neil. Later, with his newly found confidence, he nonchalantly lifted up a large black scorpion by its sting. Like the absent Don, I didn't care to risk such demonstrations, though it never bothered Joe; but then, he has reflexes like a mongoose.

We all returned to our hammocks and waited for our evening meal of rice, while Alex ground his teeth in agony at Neil's habit of chanting – at least twenty times a day and slightly off key – a snatch of a song.

'Morning has broken . . . Cannot be mended . . .'

That evening Adrian got Cham to put a call through to Georgetown for the necessary food. We learnt later that both Adrian's wife and his brother went to endless trouble, roaming round the Georgetown stores and buying large quantities of supplies for our expedition. It was no easy task, for there was a desperate shortage of certain items in the capital. At the time, I believe we never gave them sufficient credit for this unspectacular, but vital, chore.

Cham was doing his 'Zero Delta' routine and I asked

Adrian why we couldn't have an airdrop direct to Camp 6. But he didn't think that a plane would find our clearing in the present weather conditions, even if we used some of our flares, and he was determined to undertake his arduous trek, promising to get food and supplies through in a week. Until he returned, he asked Jonathan to be in charge of rationing out the food, though the climbers should take what they wanted, within reason. The climb must go on.

So it was agreed that Joe and I would go up next day to join the others, though we had no personal climbing gear. At least Mo and Mike had their boots.

Later we all stood there, queueing for our ration of rice like prisoners in a Japanese prison camp. Mosquitoes began their evening rounds – like council syphon trucks emptying the cess pools – and a large blue butterfly fluttered close by me, the first I had seen since leaving the Waruma. Some time later, several bats flitted about the camp in erratic flight.

It was while we were finishing supper that we heard a maroon rocket, but decided it was just Mo having a bit of a lark with the flares and, hoping we were right, went to bed.

We turned in that night with empty stomachs and feeling thoroughly depressed. Gloom was prevalent throughout the expedition; neither Mike nor Ragu could pursue their scientific programme properly without equipment. Lieutenant Mike and Cham were possibly the least affected by our problems since their specific tasks were mainly concerned with communications and us.

Needless to say, it was another wet night and the morning not much better. Adrian had been up since before first light, sorting out last minute details before he set off to try and reach the Paikwa trail. We had a few spoonfuls of rice and some tea made – at Ragu's suggestion – from the leaves of a palm tree. Neil acquired such a liking for this brew that, when tea eventually arrived, he still insisted on drinking the palm brew.

At 7 a.m. Adrian set off with Isaac and three Indians. He was travelling light, carrying only his small emergency bag and his long peeled stick. On his head was a wide-brimmed green hat. His socks were worn over the bottoms of his trousers to prevent insects gaining access to his legs. (As an alternative I had been wearing snow gaiters for several days and found them excellent protection.)

Jonathan presided over the thatched hut where the food was stored, like Smaug guarding his cave, and issued the day's ration to Oswald. It was meagre indeed.

By 8 a.m. we were ready to go and had five loads made up for porters. The BBC crew were coming with us, but Maurice Barrow and Mike Atherley were to follow later. They would all return to Camp 6 that same day.

Chapter 8

And many a knarled trunk was there,
   That ages long had stood,
Till time had wrought them into shapes
Like Pan's fantastic brood
Or still more foul and hideous forms
   That Pagans carve in wood ...

'The Elm Tree', *Thomas Hood*

The trail steepened a short way above Camp 6. Here the trees were noticeably smaller and, though sweat still ran from every pore like water from a sprinkling rose, it was definitely cooler than the marches on the lower trails.

Joe was just ahead of me and the BBC group took up the rear behind the porters. There was little trouble finding the trail now: it was well-marked and already a muddy trough was visible on the forest floor, churned up by the traffic to and from Camp 7.

Joe and I agreed it was good to get moving again, and we were curious to see the slime forest which must start just above.

The first ridge, though bush-covered, was quite sharp so we stopped for a breather and waited for the others to catch us up; they were not far behind. We had an occasional glimpse out over the rain forest, back in the direction of Maiurapai. The stately tree ferns were, to me, reminiscent of the West Coast of South Island in New Zealand. They were superb trees with long delicate fronds like kipper bones. Alex was first to arrive at this pleasant spot where we benefited from the occasional breeze. He looked emaciated and tired. Our expedition must have been a culinary nightmare for him: Alex loathed every item of food which we carried at the time although there was not, I admit, a very wide selection! His rice meal was punctuated by a swig of palm-leaf tea at half-time, and when there was a spoonful of sugar available, it was sprinkled on to the remaining grains of rice to make a rice pudding.

Like Alex, Gordon was wearing one of the sloppy blue bush hats which I had bought in a cheap lot at Lawrence Corner, an ex-W.D. supply store in London. His blue shirt was clean and his khaki drill slacks had only a few spots of mud on them. He wore his Nagra slung over his shoulder and was clutching his gun mike like a joiner who turns his long jack-plane upside down to remove the shavings. Alex's hand still grasped the Eclair.

'Where's blue?' I demanded.

'Struggling through the lethal swamps,' answered Gordon. 'He's not far behind.'

'Looks as if you'll get some good trail shots up here,' Joe commented. 'Should be plenty of light?'

'Well,' replied Alex, not committing himself. 'It would be almost impossible in any other place but, for here, I suppose it's a reasonable day, only nine tenths cloud cover.'

We moved on slowly, knowing that Neil would be safe in the hands of the Indians and, as Alex intended to use up some of his precious film stock on this part of the ascent, we realized that our journey to Camp 7 would not be a fast one. The terrain changed at last and suddenly became interesting; it was like flicking through the pages of a picture book on ecology: at every step, the forest was transformed. The first party to come up this ridge must have had a rough time, as it involved many detours to avoid precipitous bush-covered cliffs and there was a long double traverse on the right hand side. There were steep little chimneys, muddy and wet; and all around, moss and lichen hung down from the trees, entirely blocking our vision. Not that there was much to see since the cloud enveloped us like wet smoke.

The Indian practice of bridge-making was much in evidence; long saplings would be placed horizontally across rocky faces and anchored behind live trees on the uphill side.

These made excellent, if narrow, catwalks. Now and then vines were strategically placed as handrails, many of them speckled, resembling snakes. The thick mist embraced us clammily. It is well named the Cloud Forest or, alternatively by us, the Snot Forest. The latter was certainly appropriate at this moment as we made our first contact – literally – with the slime. It stuck to our hands and besmeared our clothes. Slime everywhere, coating the trees like axle grease.

'Hey, look at the icicle, Joe!' was my first imbecile reaction, although I realized almost immediately that it hadn't been cold enough for frost the previous night. It was indeed just like an icicle, beautifully tapered and suspended from a twig, it was clear as gelatine.

We saw our first pitcher plants (Heliamphora nutans) growing in clumps; their mouths open like fledglings, ready to catch any falling drops of rain or unwary insects.

The face was steep now and we progressed by pulling ourselves from branch to branch. The small trees were contorted fantastically: one particular branch described a complete circle, forming a loop eighteen feet in diameter, before growing outwards a further few yards. Alex was busy filming while Joe and I behaved like kids who had been let loose in a toy shop or, as I then recollected, like the time in San Francisco when we spent several hours in a Chinese store which contained all the fabulous puzzles and games of the Orient.

The hillside seemed over-populated; every plant struggling for the best position. Great fat bromeliads, like pineapples with a 'high profile', flower only once in their lifetime. Bladderworts (Utricularias), like sweetpeas, grew up to three feet in height from the leaf axils of the bromeliads. There were sedges and liverworts besides, and weird and wonderful small trees, some with leaves which resembled uninflated football bladders. For the first time since leaving Maiurapai, there was a feeling of space, of freedom to move. Although we were still amongst the compact stunted Bonnetia, we could see out over the rain forest when the cloud cleared, which it did more frequently now: I think we had more or less climbed up through it.

'You know, Joe,' I remarked, swinging myself up on a short, slimy branch. 'I think this is fabulous – I wouldn't have missed it for all the scorpions in the rain forest!'

'You should see all the things inside this bromeliad,' said Joe, peering into it intently. 'It's like a tiny community: all sorts of bugs and insects.'

At 6,700 feet there is a notch on the ridge, above which is a steep cliff clad with a profusion of greenery. Here Mike and Mo had slung a rope ladder. Whilst climbing it, we became completely plastered in mud (I can appreciate now what it must have been like in the trenches of the First World War). We had a breather at the top and I went back down the slimy rungs to collect Alex's camera as he found it impossible to climb the pitch and carry the camera.

Like Theseus escaping from the Labyrinth, we made our way through one final extra dense and black, greasy thicket, and emerged on relatively open ground. Not ground as one normally imagines it, however, but a series of small pools set in white, sticky sand on a 20° slope: this was El Dorado swamp. An unbelievable place which might have come straight out of *The Day of the Triffids*. The ridge was flatter here and sloped easily down, on our left, to the headwaters of the Paikwa river. We knew that, just beyond our field of vision, an abrupt escarpment fell 1,000 feet; farther along and just visible to us, superb waterfalls shot out and over this vertical drop, never touching it. A green belt of forest extended now to the great cliff wall of Roraima, still masked by cloud. On our right the ridge fell away in another cliff, almost vertical for 1,500 feet, down to the forest which bounds the north-west face of the mountain.

We were up to our ankles in this white, oozing mud, but used the great matted pitcher plants as stepping stones, the rain-diluted acid from the pitchers spurting out as we stood on them. There were scarlet sundews too, the hairs of their plump leaves tipped with a sticky exudate for trapping insects. Moss hung like hideous wigs from the branches of the bushes.

There was a crashing in the bush ahead of us: Mo burst upon us suddenly. He was dressed only in his longjohns and boots. His Karrimor rucksack was slung over his shoulder and he looked pale and drawn.

'Hello there,' he greeted us briefly.

'You going down?' asked Joe.

'No fags,' Mo replied in disgust.

'Completely out?'

'Yes.'

'Well, nothing's come up to 6,' said Joe. 'You're wasting your time going down.'

'Oh, I'll go right down until I get them,' Mo answered. 'I can't climb without cigs.'

'Did you send off a distress flare last night?' I asked.

'Yes,' he replied. 'Quite a bloody bang – did you hear it echoing round the cliffs?'

'Didn't we just,' said Joe indignantly. 'We might have been up in the middle of the night if the route hadn't been so bad!'

'We didn't think you'd be that dedicated,' Mo laughed. 'We were only wondering what had happened to you. Anyhow, I'll be seeing you – I'll bribe the Indians to get the fags, even if it means going to Georgetown!'

I walked on through the fairyland as though in a dream. Alex brought me sharply back to reality:

'If you two wait here for ten minutes, Gordon and I can go ahead and film your arrival at Camp 7.'

'Righto,' Joe agreed easily. 'Don't hang about though; it looks as if it's about to piss those spears which are called raindrops in this part of the world.'

Mike, Don and Maurice were all standing in front of the

shelter when we arrived at Camp 7. Alex and Gordon were discreetly ensconced on one side, filming furiously. We went through the long-time-no-see routine for posterity ...

A sudden clearing in the cloud and, for about half a minute, the Prow came into view: breathtaking grandeur. We gazed at it, spellbound. The rock seemed to rise up and up without any respite; we couldn't see even a ledge on it. Then it was gone; once more a wall of cloud and the show was over. Alex was disgusted. He hadn't even had time to point his camera.

The boys had built a shelter in a clump of Bonnetia, whose tortured and twisted trunks grew all awry. To the south-east – the windward side – a wall of bushes had been built up to protect the inmates from driving rain. A short 'canal' (the path) led away from the shelter to a partial clearing. Mud was everywhere and came over the tops of our boots. Maurice made a cup of tea for us, our first for many hours, and Alex and I shared a packet of Opal Mints which tasted wonderful. It looked as if we would be better off here than at Camp 6.

Forty feet from the shelter on the crest of the ridge was a step – wet, naturally, but reasonably level and clear of bushes. This was to have served as our helipad and would have been quite adequate for that purpose. We had already told Mo the bad news about the helicopter, but now Mike and Don learnt of it.

'There's no one you can call on for a pair of climbing boots, is there, Hamish?' asked Mike. Joe and Don would be able to double up with Mo and Mike, but I was size 9. I'd have to use my cane cutter's boots, though I didn't fancy that very much. At least we had enough climbing gear to keep going for a few days. Mo and Mike had been working away at the Wall and we still had quite a lot of fixed rope, with more down at Camp 6. In fact most of the climbing gear was already in; it was just the personal stuff that we were missing. I didn't fancy climbing without a harness, though. Mike,

1   Joe relaxes

2   Don kept his matches dry

3   Adrian with Isaac Jerry

4   Mike Atherley gets in some target practice

'Always a little further' – Neil

The author in his hammock

7   Maurice, Don and Mike Thompson at Camp 7,
                        Joe looking out of his mosquito net

8   Mud and water at the El Dorado Swamp

9   Loading the canoes at Kamarang

View of the Prow from Camp 6. Adrian is in the foreground

11   Joe in the slime forest with a bromeliad and a
bladderwork in the foreground

Camp 8: Alex Scott with the camera, the author in the hammock, Mo in the foreground

Don jumars up the fixed rope on the Great Roof

Mo standing on top of the Prow, looking down towards
El Dorado Swamp in the centre of the photograph

17

The author climbing the overhanging chimney on the last day

18

The summit plateau: Mo and Joe are on the other side of the sunken garden

19　' "Will you have a cigarette, mate?" said the Leader
of the Push.' The view from El Dorado Swamp

20   Looking vertically down the Big Corner between my
cane cutter's boots at Don on the Cabbage Patch

21

Mo on the edge of the Africa Flake

22

Roraima after a night's rain

23

Moving out on the fixed rope on the Great Roof,
a tarantula's-eye-view from the Terrace

24

'Helmets' in the sunken gardens on the summit of
Mount Roraima

who like Mo had taken the precaution of bringing most of his climbing things in with him, said I could borrow his. Their problem was not having a change of clothes. It was quite dry up on the face, but they said they got soaked commuting!

'Well, I'm going to cut a new trail to the shithouse,' said Don with determination. 'I'm fed up with struggling over and under those branches. It's like weaving in and out of the rungs of a ladder.'

I visited the clearing later to see how he was getting on; it was almost as big as the helipad and a respectable 200 feet away from the shelter. When the cloud lifted it must have been one of the most scenic bogs in the world!

Don's cutlass was clanging away on the iron-hard wood when Neil arrived at camp with two of the Indians. (The others had caught us up earlier.) He came into sight round a small bush with a wisp of moss hanging from it looking like a tattered distress flag which had been hopefully hoisted many years before.

' "We travel not for trafficking alone, by hotter winds our fiery hearts are fanned",' Neil quoted Flecker as if he had just moved out from the wings. ' "For lust of knowing what should not be known, we take the Golden road to Samarkand." '

In reply I took liberties with 'Hassan':

' "When softly through the Trongate beat the bells, along the London Road to Barrowland ... That's an old Scottish version, Neil!' I explained as he raised his hand in acknowledgement.

'That climb was gruelling, blue,' Neil commented, wading through the deep mud like a paddy coolie. He looked tired and fed-up; I think he was hurt that we hadn't waited for him.

I was continually astounded afresh by Neil's generosity. He was now without a pullover – he'd given his to Don – and didn't have a sleeping bag, for Cham's one was useless so

Neil had lent him his own. He had donated his spare socks to one of the Indians and, though more-or-less a chain smoker, had refused cigarettes when they were scarce, as at this time. Now, when offered food by the Indian, Maurice, he simply wouldn't take it, saying we climbers would want all the grub there was to get up the Wall.

His chief worry was the continuing cloud, the impossibility of getting good pictures of the Prow, and the real need to get the camera crew installed at Camp 7 before we climbers all disappeared up the face. Alex looked pale (nothing, he assured me, a few ten-course meals wouldn't fix), but he said he had the 70 DR camera and about 500 feet of film at Camp 6 and I could take this on with me if I wanted. I thought it might be a bit heavy to climb with. The sooner Adrian got back with the small autoload cameras the better. I didn't think I could change the film for the bigger camera up on the face.

A loud coo-ee heralded the arrival of Maurice Barrow and Mike Atherley. Maurice carried his cine camera, as if it was a live parcel-bomb, and Mike was unladen except for the automatic pistol which he always wore in his holster. Mike refused the spaghetti, but Maurice gulped down a portion at great speed, as though scared it might vanish like worms beneath the mud.

The hammocks were strung across the shelter: that the place would be overcrowded was a gross understatement, I thought. As it was, the Indian, Maurice, had slept under the hammock supports the previous night. With Joe and me to swell the company, it would be like a writhing nest of snakes. I commented about the overcrowding to Mike; he agreed with me but thought Mo was going to bring one of the small Bukta tents up and pitch it on a raft of brushwood in the swamp.

Mike Thompson's shoes were in a terrible state; they were only made of light canvas (he never received his cane cutter boots – these items seemed to be spirited away like the food in the jungle) and his toes stuck out of one. In the meantime, the rents in his shirt seemed to have multiplied.

Joe asked him how the climb was going.

'Quite good,' replied Mike unexpansively. 'The rock's much better than we ever imagined.'

It was extremely cold at Camp 7 and Maurice was working over the Gaz stove in the 'kitchen', wearing Mike's duvet jacket.

Two loud cracks outside indicated that Mike Atherley was practising with his automatic. Neil went out and had a go, too. He used to be a fair shot with a pistol, as he played a lead role in a series on the Mafia and had to use a pistol for some of the takes.

The Indians squatted at the edge of the clearing for a time; then decided to return to Camp 6, and as the cloud didn't look like shifting, Neil went with them. They started off down in small straggling groups. Their boots made sucking noises, like kids eating lollipops, in the thick white mud. I wandered over to the couple of murky pools we got our water from on the other side of the clearing and decided to occupy myself by deepening them, using an empty tin as a dredger. Meanwhile, Joe and Mike fixed a section of yellow tarpaulin (which we had brought with us) over the exposed thatched gable end, to try to keep out the driving rain. Don had his hammock slung the far side of the shelter on the other flank; when the wind changed a couple of days later, he received a terrific soaking.

The clanking of Don's cutlass had ceased and a few minutes later he came into the shelter by the 'back door' (the route to the toilet). He was stripped to the waist and bathed in sweat, but smug with achievement. He had spent all the previous day fixing a couple of hundred feet of the green corlene to lash the twisted limbs together so that in their united form, strengthened by rope guys angling down to the roots of their fellows, a sturdy structure had been established.

'Hey, the peak's clear,' Mike announced from the clearing. The whole mountain was sharply defined against a grey cloud, naked and red in the late afternoon light.

'What a sight,' I said, again overawed by the incredible shape of the rock. Over twenty-five square miles of it. I'd never seen anything like it.

'Aye, it's not a bad wee mountain,' admitted Don; he had a pair of miniature binoculars with him and now he scrutinized the Prow. He could see Mike's rope quite easily.

The day before, Mo and Mike had got to the small ledge, covered with bromeliads, about 150 feet up. It had looked harder going above, because there was more vegetation on the next section. But they had found a fantastic place to bivvy at the bottom of the Wall which would save us over an hour of rough going between where we were then and the base of the Prow. We wouldn't even need to take a tent because once we'd cleared some big sandstone slabs from the ledge it would be a sort of natural cave with a rock roof. If we pegged a tarpaulin around it, it would make a nice little shelter.

One of the pitches Mo had led was vertical mud, so they'd fixed a rope on it, but warned us we'd have to use jumar clamps to climb it, as the mud made the rope slippery to grasp, and with a rucksack it would be too steep to climb hand over hand anyway.

Just then Mo arrived in camp, carrying a big rucksack. He was still sadly fagless, but had brought up some more food and odds and ends of climbing gear and a tent which he proceeded to put up – to give his back a change of position, he said. For many years Mo, as well as Joe, has been troubled with his back; it is a constant worry for them both.

The others had reached Camp 6 about the same time as Mo arrived back at 7. They were all tired and Alex felt his leg muscles sore. Oswald had carried up to Camp 7 for us and had had nothing to eat since morning, but Jonathan refused to give him any rice when he came in. Oswald was both angry and hungry when he went to bed that night.

With our priority rations, we had a good meal, and were chatting contentedly when the rain started. Lower down, in the rain forest, although the rain was torrential, a lot of the impact was absorbed by the forest canopy. There was no such protection here and it beat down with such ferocity that we wondered if it would sever the stout flysheet. Water foamed through the shelter in channels in the mud, and there was no need to wash the dishes – we just left them outside for a few minutes and they were spotlessly clean. Our water bucket would fill as rapidly as it might from a fireman's hose, yet it was only catching the water shed from part of the flysheet.

'The new fortifications seem to be all right,' Mo observed, looking up at the flysheet lashed round the end of the shelter. I fervently hoped so.

The first of the large black mosquitoes made their appearance: great big blighters with probes like blunt hypodermics. They were quite the biggest I had ever seen. There were lots of huge butterflies and a few humming birds, possibly the green Roraima emerald, known only to this area. Occasionally a covey of parakeets, green and fast-flying, would pass overhead, chattering away and manoeuvring in perfect unison like a well-trained fighter squadron.

The rain eased off so Mo dashed out to build a pier for his tent. I had misgivings about using a tent in this climate, which was why I had postponed my judgement till the morrow. He was back in twenty minutes, having accomplished the task to his satisfaction.

Over a brew of hot conny milk – the tea was finished – we planned the next day's programme, as Don trimmed his beard. Mo favoured a day off after climbing the first section and doing the return trip through the bush. So it was agreed Joe and Mike would go on the wall, and because I still had no climbing boots, I volunteered to improve the trail to the face with Don. If there was time I was also keen to try and get to the bottom of the great waterfall that feeds into the headwaters of the Paikwa. Isaac had once tried to cut across to it, but no one had yet reached there and I was convinced it was a good place for diamonds.

'Sounds interesting,' said Don speculatively.

Our hammocks were a haven in that sea of mud; once inside the mosquito net, one gained a sense of security and, as Mo had remarked earlier on, we were like parrots. When the mosquito nets were draped over, conversation generally ceased – sometimes as early as 6.45 p.m. – though we would often read by torchlight, each net gleaming like a chrysalid. Don didn't read much so he usually sorted out some gear and would, from time to time, come out with a well-prepared remark. He had spent some time that evening examining the face and the edge of the precipice before the rain made further viewing impossible.

'You know what I'd like to do?' he said. 'Come back with Audrey one day, and just walk round the edge of that plateau.'

'Could be an interesting trip,' I agreed.

'Just a holiday trip, you know,' he continued. 'Up by the tourist route from Venezuela and spend a few days at a camp on the summit.'

'Adrian was saying that they're going to run conducted tours to the summit, from Venezuela,' I remarked.

'Aye, I heard that, but it's not in my line.'

Maurice was again slung under the cross support and a stream of water now splashed into the bucket, from the edge of the flysheet, about three inches away from his face. For the past ten minutes the bucket had been overflowing.

'Still dry, Maurice?' Joe asked.

'Yes,' Maurice laughed. 'Very wet place, Camp 7.'

'Aye, you'll be wanting to get back to your cassava patch,' said Don.

Night shift had started: the mosquitoes had been busy for some time, but now large luminous insects winged their way into the shelter, like tube trains arriving at a platform. Some were amazingly bright. Joe caught several, but Maurice was by far the best at catching insects and butterflies. His reactions were incredibly fast and he would pick the swiftest flying insect out of the air, or off a plant, with nonchalant ease.

We all slept soundly that night – which is unusual in the jungles of Guyana. One can expect to be awakened half a dozen times by unusual noises, or in order to fend off some insect which has breached the defences.

Dawn was startlingly clear. It was as if the deluge of the previous night had, by its sheer volume of water, washed away all the cloud. The great tabletop of rock looked as if it had been wirebrushed overnight and the waterfalls, tumbling a clear 1,500 feet, were like cream. It was pleasant to be able to take one's allocation of toilet roll, which spun on a cut-off branch, and meander up the 'Rue de Whillans' where, amidst the pineapple plants, one could gaze without care (except for creepy-crawlies) at the great cliff. The other peaks were visible that morning, sparkling clean: Maringma, Weiassipu, Kukenaam, Eluwarima, Waikepaipe, mesas looming like a convoy of aircraft carriers. The rain forest spread out like a rich carpet, the even pile disturbed only by the indentations of the Waruma and Paikwa Rivers. The first great waterfall – the one Don and I were interested in – fell directly from the Roraima cliff into what looked like a great basin, gouged out by millions of years of water erosion. Then it disappeared into the dense belt of vegetation which skirts the main cliffs of the mountain and lower escarpment. But, just above the point where the water plunges over the lower escarpment in a superb cataract, there seemed to be another pool. The previous night Don had suggested that we should scout the cliffs for another possible ascent line near this waterfall, but Mo maintained that the Prow was the best bet. When Mike and he had first reached the base of the Prow, they had traversed leftwards, as John Streetly and Bev Clark had done, to try and gain a large overhanging groove. Mo had, as it transpired, rightly decided against trying to climb it since the exit from it, higher up the cliff, looked both difficult and dangerous. He had chosen a route which, had a plumb line been suspended from the highest point of the Prow, would have followed the line faithfully for three-quarters of the way up the face.

Mike was the self-appointed cook at Camp 7 but, unfortunately, Mo decided to make the porridge that morning. He was engrossed in relating some story and neglected to stir the lethal concoction, with the result that it was almost uneatable.

'Never mind, Don,' said Mo laughing, 'it's better than descaling a boiler in Sheffield!'

Joe had just caught a weird insect which we called the JCB: it had two digger-like instruments on its front legs which looked as if they could only be used for digging parallel drains.

'Some of these insects are all prick and ribs,' observed Mo with interest. 'Can I borrow your Welli boots today, Hamish?'

'Sure,' I said. 'But don't let the mud get inside.'

I had taken the precaution of carrying my pair of calf-length thermal boots with me from Maiurapai; they proved very useful in this swampy ground.

We set off at intervals each carrying a load of rope, Don and I taking up the rear. Though the cloud had closed in again, it was interesting walking up the ridge. Above El Dorado swamp, the country becomes bushier again and, where it steepens, the ridge also becomes more defined. By the time we reached the final step below the bottom of the Wall, we were on a narrow crest with a drop of about 2,000 feet to our right.

The Bonnetia was even more twisted here, like metal cuttings from a lathe. Some of the bromeliads were enormous, up to six feet high, and when we accidentally brushed against one on the trail, the contents – often many gallons of water – would be generously poured all over us. There were some very steep steps here and, from time to time, we had to climb up tree branches to surmount a short wall of mud and slime. It was impossible to keep clean; in no time we were coated in mud and soaked through, dripping with both water and sweat.

We took a breather where the ridge levelled out again. Don drove his cutlass into a branch as he sat down and it gave a twang, as if he had tried to cut a steel hawser. Our route to the waterfall would be along the ridge to the left. We decided to dump some of the rope at the awkward places as we climbed; this would save us some energy and we could fix it on the way back in the afternoon. I sorted out a hundred feet or so, and promised to fix the worst bit, the section above that steep wall at the end of the ridge when I came down from the face.

A single rope hung down the mud face which we encountered at the end of the ridge. We took out our climbing clamps and fixed them securely to this mud-blackened rope. One at a time, we moved up the rope, sliding first one clamp, then the other, and taking our weight alternatively on each. The clamps have nylon tape stirrups attached to them and can only move one way. Their use greatly facilitates the ascent of treacherous or overhanging terrain, provided there is a fixed rope.

Another ten minutes and we were at the base of the Prow. 'I'm here at last,' I thought. 'This is what it's all about.' The rock rose up and out above my head so that only the first great roof was visible. On the steep wall of vegetation bromeliads were leaning out from the cliff face at strategic places, in order to catch the drips from above; it was dry close in to the bottom of the face. The bivouac ledge was, as Mike had indicated, superb.

Joe and Mike were sorting out their equipment. Already they were wearing their climbing harness and helmets.

'Saw a couple of nasty looking spiders here just now,' said Joe. 'Got red arses like circus clowns.'

'I saw a big bird-eating spider at the bottom of the steep mud face,' Mike added as he clipped some karabiners on to his harness. 'It didn't seem too friendly.'

I left them the rope and went back down to join Don to continue our explorations.

'Don't forget to share any loot with your friends,' was Joe's parting remark. 'Since we're doing all the work anyhow.'

I quickly fixed rope on the steep section as I descended, and was back with Don in about twenty minutes.

'Got this cutlass fine and sharp now, Hamish; could almost shave with it.'

'Hey, look at that humming bird!'

A superb bird was hovering just a few feet away from me, staring inquisitively. It reminded me of the Harrier vertical take-off fighter. One moment stationary; the next, away like a bat out of hell. We found the start of Isaac's trail and followed it, Don leading the way, cutting secondary growth which had sprung up since 1971.

There are some places that I have visited which remain in my mind like half-forgotten snatches of a tune: the Cuillin Ridge in Skye on a February day; a lonely valley in the Himalaya where my only companions were a couple of bears (some distance away) and that idyllic path, skirting under the 1,500 feet high red sandstone cliffs of Roraima, was unforgettable. Both Don and I felt the same. It was like a lost paradise, albeit a sightly hostile one. There was a galaxy of flowers, and long ferns made intricate tracery against the red rock and birds mocked at us, and one was so close that I could almost touch it.

I gave Don a spell up front, taking his cutlass. I had only gone a short way when I found a long and narrow clearing ahead of me: a corridor about twenty feet wide, running along the bottom of the vertical Wall. 'In the name of the wee man, Don, look at this! Have you ever seen anything like it?'

He too, gazed in disbelief.

'A ruddy cabbage avalanche!'

It was an avalanche tip of bromeliads. Big ones, small ones, every shape and size; it looked as if the unsaleable cabbage crop of a bankrupt market gardener had been dumped along the bottom of the face. They were many feet deep and as we walked over them, strange noises stole out as if they were alive and in pain. We trod along those great 'fruits' of the mesa like athletic grape treaders.

'I suppose they must fall off the Wall,' I said lamely, stating the obvious since the Georgetown refuse collectors would hardly dump their booty here! I craned my neck to gaze at the forbidding overhangs above me. Bromeliads sprouted everywhere; every suspicion of a crack or hand-hold seemed to offer a home to a number of bromeliads.

These bromeliads are hardy plants, but the enormous compost heap made it plain that some of their homes had been precarious indeed. The cabbage avalanche extended for about a hundred yards and then the bush became impossibly dense. I tried forcing a way through right under the face which now had veins of jasper-like rock running through it, but it was little better there. The angle of the rock above was so steep that we had had the impression that the 'green belt' was lying at an easy angle. In fact, it was really steep and, as I slanted down slightly, I found that I was on branches about seven foot above ground level. My arms ached with cutting the iron-hard wood and the cutlass rapidly lost its edge. The sap from the bushes exuded a deep red substance, almost as if they were bleeding. Don was watching my antics from behind and followed in the 'channel' which I cut.

'I suppose one could describe this as an air corridor, Don?'

'Want a spell?'

I handed him the blunted machete gratefully:

'It's all yours, mate! "As the creeper that girdles the tree-trunk," ' I quoted from my Kipling. ' "The Law runneth forward and back – for the strength of the Pack is the Wolf, and the strength of the Wolf is the Pack." '

'Aye, here, take this bleeding pack; it gets in the way,' Don set to and attacked the forest in a wave of destruction.

It was fast becoming ridiculous. We were moving like spastic baboons suffering from arthritis, now ten feet above the ground, liable to end our days at any moment, impaled on the lancer-like saplings which we cut at the most convenient angle (about 45°) but which we also knew was probably the optimum angle for penetrating the human body!

'I think we'll have to forget the waterfall for today, don't you, Don?' I spoke from the depths of a hole. I was clinging to two branches which had fortunately acted like a lifebelt for my arms as I slipped down.

'Aye, I don't think we're going to get much further, lad. Perhaps if we go back to the main trail we could try at a lower level?'

'I saw a ruddy great chasm down there,' I replied. 'It could take a week with a party of Indians to reach that waterfall.'

I quoted, appropriately enough, from Longfellow's 'Hiawatha's Friends':

> 'Till they found all further passage
> Shut against them, barred securely
> By the trunks of trees uprooted
> Lying lengthwise, lying crosswise,
> And forbidding further passage.'

'Your passage will be blocked one of these days with all that crap you spout,' he pronounced ominously. We agreed we would try to get back later on to this marvellous spot and turned our attention to the line above. Don pointed out a crack system to the left of the Prow, some 200 feet up the Wall. But there was an extra 300 feet or so of climbing there, compared to the Prow. The escarpment leading up to the Prow gained that bit of extra height.

We made our way back to the main trail again just as the cloud came down and it started to drizzle. Back on the narrow ridge, we ate some peanuts and sucked an Opal Mint apiece. I gathered up the rope I had left there and put it in my rucksack. Then we headed down, cutting off some of the sharp spikes lower down on which we'd nearly put our eyes out on the way up. Taking turn about, we started to enlarge and improve the trail, hacking away at the giant bromeliads – I felt as if I was chopping up tough old ladies in crinolines.

Glancing back during a temporary lifting of the cloud, we saw Joe and Mike. Don gave one of his piercing whistles which echoed from the crag like a ricocheting bullet. Joe, equally adept, replied in kind.

'Looks hard that, Don.'

'Oh, I doubt if any of it's easy,' he replied, his eyes forming tiny slits as he stared up. 'We've got our work cut out over the next few weeks.'

I had blistered my hands using the cutlass so I went on down to camp. Don said he would take his time and watch the lads and finish off the trail back to camp.

As I squelched down, from one wet footstep to the next, trying not to touch the vegetation which was all either slimy or prickly, I was glancing in front (as one does automatically in climbing) to the footholds I would use a couple of steps ahead; the steps close to hand having been subconsciously examined and filed in the memory bank. I did happen to sense a movement just as my foot was coming down on a wet muddy foothold. But it was too late, for my 'automatic pilot' was busy computing a slippery branch growing along the ground about three feet farther on. The movement I caught out of the corner of my eye was caused by three snakes which were curled up on the mud, obviously trying to get a blink of the sun which had just emerged. Size 9

Bata sugar cane cutter's boots crunched down heavily on top of them and I continued past and had reached the slippery branch before I could check my forward momentum. The snakes were only small, each about six inches long, and were obviously more scared than me, as they wasted no time in hanging about!

Mo had seen me coming and had a milk brew on; he also

karabiner

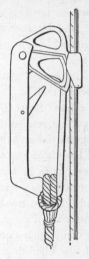

jumar clamp

offered me some cold rice, which I probably loathe almost as much as Alex, since it had formed my staple diet for three months during the previous year. I said I'd settle for a bit of tuna fish instead, even if it did taste like pulverized purple heart.

Mo had a flare ready, just in case the helicopter came, but 'waiting for spares' could mean anything.

That day was an easy one for the party at Camp 6. The BBC group were tired and stiff after their climb to El Dorado swamp. They discussed how they might carry their equipment up to our camp, as there were no porters left at Camp 6. They concluded that it wasn't possible in their present physical condition; besides their personal gear, there was a mass of filming and recording equipment which was far too heavy for them to move on their own. There was nothing else to do but wait until porters arrived with supplies. There was now only a few days' food left in camp. Cham caught a large black scorpion near his radio transmitter, however, and it was given to Mike Tamessar for his collection.

Chapter 9

And the rain descended, and the floods came,
and the wind blew, and beat upon that house;
and it fell not: for it was founded upon a rock.

Matthew 7:25

We had now reached the stage of the expedition where serious climbing would commence, and Joe, spending his first day on the Prow with Mike Thompson, was experiencing climbing of a nature unknown to him. Scorpions and spiders were the problems now to be faced!

While Don and I were proceeding to the Diamond Waterfall, like Christian and Hopeful en route for the Celestial City, Joe was cleaning his jumars and preparing to follow Mike up the fixed rope which hung down by the cave, not touching the Wall.

Mike had completed the first pitch, the first part of which was 150 feet overhanging. This brought him to the Niche, a ledge some three feet square, reached by a narrow shelf leading from the top of the fixed rope. The rope was attached at the bottom of the face to prevent one swinging out too far, and also to guide us back into the cave when descending, otherwise our landing would be in a bed of bromeliads, tilted at an angle of 60°. Doubtless, this was a fruitful source for the 'compost heap' three hundred feet below. This 'allotment' ended abruptly on the brink of a red rock wall which dropped smoothly down to where Don and I were.

Joe soon discovered that the rock was excellent, Mo and Mike had made no idle boast. The first pitch really started with a bang; it reared up like the bows of a huge ocean liner, up and over a rock roof on to the steep face. For most of the ascent Joe was jumaring clear of the rock.

There are several methods of using jumar clamps. The simplest way to explain the technique is to visualize nylon tape loops attached to the clamps; the shorter loop is clipped on to the climbing harness at waist level, so that one can hang comfortably from it once the clamp is attached to the fixed rope. The other sling – or stirrup – is used for the foot and the clamp reaches about waist level on the fixed rope. In order to move, the waist loop clamp is moved up first: then one leans backwards from this to enable the lower clamp to be slid up the rope until it almost touches the top one. This process is repeated and height is gained by standing up on the stirrup; it is strenuous work and the sling lengths are critical. There are more sophisticated systems in use employing various slings, but to explain them would be like trying to describe the differential gear without moving one's hands.

Soon Joe had joined Mike. Later, he told me his first impressions:

The pitch above looked reasonably short, a fairly wide open groove full of vegetation. I could see, to the left of this groove, a slightly overhanging crack, tapering as it got higher. This too had its bits and pieces of greenery in it. Mike safeguarded me with the rope as I set off, for I wanted first to go round to the right to see if there was an easier way. But it looked hard and unprotected I discovered, so I returned and started up the crack.

It was almost completely artificial climbing. I used an assortment of pitons for the first half, then holds started to appear. As I cleaned these using the spike of the piton hammer, I unearthed scorpions and some really nasty looking insects. This, of course, made quite a difference to feeling relaxed. Instead of being able to reach up and use holds as I would normally have done, I had to climb up so that I could inspect them before pulling up, in case I got stung. In the end, I used more pegs than usual because of this danger.

At sixty feet above Mike, the rock became loose and the good crack began to fade. It was a bit dangerous. I was about fifteen feet from a big ledge which I was aiming for and could see a great overhang of bromeliads, like the headfeathers of an Indian chief, guarding the edge. There was nowhere to put a peg and I was tiring with the strain of the insecurity, as well as the fear of being bitten, so I shouted down to Mike: 'I'm coming down; I've had enough for one day.'

Their tally for the day was two spiders and six scorpions. Mike saw one beside a bromeliad which was growing on the Niche; in a flash he had smashed it with his peg hammer but the ground was so resilient that the irate spider escaped and hid under the foliage. As they abseiled off, both climbers were alarmed to hear creaking noises from the corlene rope. As Joe remarked later:

'My life, to me, is worth an extra rope – I'll put another fixed rope in place tomorrow.'

Doing a rapid mental calculation as to the amount of corlene and ordinary climbing rope still spare, I reckoned we should have enough to put double rope up the whole route, and if we did that we could have a spare jumar clamp running on the safety rope as we went up, to double the safety factor. There've been too many people killed on their single fixed ropes.

Down at Camp 6, Alex was feeling rotten: he had a terrible cold and snuffled miserably all night as the rain hammered defiantly against the flysheet. Maurice 'the Spy' and Mike Tamessar got soaked by the driving rain which blew under the bottom end of the shelter.

I slept that night in one of the small Bukta tents, which proved to be amazingly waterproof, though it sounded as if I were incarcerated in one of Mo's Sheffield boilers while the riveters were hard at work outside.

The programme for the following day – 18 October – was that Don and I would fix rope on the steep parts of the trail to the face, and Mo and Joe would climb. Mike was to stay at camp for his off day.

Mo went on ahead. The morning was unbelievable; the mountain was as clear as we had seen it yet, blood red in the morning light and not a wisp of cloud to be seen, except that perpetually hanging over the rain forest. Joe was up ahead of me and the parakeets performed their morning manoeuvres.

'Hey, look at this, Hamish.' I had caught up with Joe and he held up a snake he had captured. He gripped it between finger and thumb close to its head.

'You'd better watch it,' I warned. 'It may be lethal.'

'Oh, it can't get away,' he assured me, though the creature was whipping back and forwards like the tail of an outraged cat. All the same, he agreed to rest its head on a handy branch and let me decapitate it with the edge of my hammer. A couple of blows and it was quite dead. We didn't know what kind it was but didn't want to take the risk of letting it go free, in case someone was later bitten by it. The Indians kill dangerous snakes when they can, and so does Adrian; it is good policy although none of us would have killed anything unnecessarily.

I accompanied Joe to the bottom of the Wall, as I was taking some rope up for the climbers, and Don followed behind. The route to the Prow was fraught with difficulties for it involved some of the steepest bush climbing of the whole march. The undergrowth was unbelievably dense, multi-coloured, and twisting and twining in all directions; it reminded me of the interior of a complicated piece of electronic equipment. The work which Don and I had carried out the previous day certainly speeded things up, but a multitude of short, steep, muddy and root-infested pitches required fixed rope to enable us to climb with our heavy rucksacks. I had taken enough rope with me to safeguard these sections, as well as the 200 feet which Mo and Joe needed. Don was carrying up more climbing gear, pitons and bongs – large U-sectioned pieces of alloy or steel up to four inches in width, which, when hammered into cracks as climbing aids, emit a resounding 'bong-bong', not far removed from the euphonic note of a Tyrolean cow bell.

The sixty feet pitch up a vertical mud bank which we had encountered the previous day was really revolting. Even if you succeeded in keeping reasonably clean from the waist up before clipping jumars to the black, slimy rope, by the time five feet had been accomplished through the well worn channel to the first mud overhang, you were covered with slime. This also clogged the teeth of our jumars.

Mo had arrived at the Cave and was struggling into his Whillans climbing harness.

'I'm going to leave my climbing boots up here today,' he told me. 'I'm fed-up with getting them filled with mud. I've brought my old jungle bashing shoes up with me.'

It was certainly dry enough just there under the overhang, and a sensible roof under which to establish camp.

'We must have chosen the worst commuting area in the world,' Joe commented on arrival. 'An hour and a half of wet, muddy hell before you can even start the day's work!'

'Plus the vertical footage, which will be increasing daily ...' I added, gazing up the rope which disappeared out of sight some fifty feet above us.

Mo went smoothly up the fixed rope. Don and I lingered to take photographs before we went back down. In the following account, Joe describes his day's climbing fortunes:

We quickly reached the highest point of the day before. This time I had taken a pocketful of self-drilling bolts. These bolts have teeth round the rim at one end which, when hammered, bite into the rock; this saves using a separate drill for making the hole. However, they couldn't have been well-tempered for, when I started to hammer them, they quickly blunted and the teeth burred over. I knew that the rock was incredibly hard but the bolts must still have been faulty. It took twelve to drill a single hole and, standing in stirrups from a lower peg – as I was – it was tiring work. When I finally fixed the bolt, I didn't trust it so, looking about, I found a tiny crack into which I put a small knife-blade peg. Carefully, I moved up on this peg, rather than risk using the bolt. I had now reached a very narrow ledge which was really awkward to get on to because of the great bromeliads. They were too big to pull off – about four feet high and like huge pine cones – and yet not strong enough to pull up on.

After a struggle I stood up but, before I could traverse to reach a large platform, I had to move fifteen feet to my right, where the small ledge I was now on tapered and faded on to a blank wall. The climbing was very difficult and I eventually put in a RURP [Realized Ultimate Reality Piton. Its persistent use could lead to premature heart failure, or the physical destruction of a climber; its holding power is definitely more psychological than real] – a tiny piton of high quality nickel steel, about the length of a finger joint.

I gently clinched the RURP between my forefinger and thumb, and just managed to step across to the big ledge. Above me I saw a prominent feature of the climb which we had studied from below: the great corner which we later called the Big Diedre. Don christened the large ledge, the Cabbage Patch, as it boasted a prolific crop of bromeliads, like a pineapple plantation; what it lacked in area it compensated for by the gargantuan size of its products.

'Can I come up now?' Mo eventually shouted impatiently from the Niche.

'I don't see any point, Mo – I'll clean out the route when I abseil down; I'm at the foot of the big corner now.'

'Okay,' Mo shouted back, sounding bored.

In fact, he didn't really have such a boring day on the Niche: it was enlivened by a six-inch long millipede heading towards him down the face, and frequent spiky cushion plants which hurtled past, knocked down by Joe. The vast amount of energy expended that day had only gained Joe, and the expedition, seven feet, in vertical height, but it was seven critical feet: the bottom of the Big Diedre had been successfully reached and Joe felt it would 'go' without too much trouble. We felt optimistic about the first section, at least.

As the cloud had descended upon this particular act of the Lost World drama, Don and I didn't see much of the day's vertical play. We fixed rope hand-rails along the path, gradually working our way back down to Camp 7. Meanwhile, down at Camp 6, at about the time that Don and I arrived back at Camp 7 and Mo and Joe were starting their abseil off, Cham had a radio message from his colleague at Maiurapai. Adrian had arrived there the day before; he had done the trip in one and a half days. An astounding feat. We learnt of his safe arrival the same evening via Maurice who had gone down to Camp 6 that morning and returned laden with Gaz cylinders and climbing gear, bringing a note from Neil.

Joe got a Gaz light going and Maurice and Mike made our evening meal by its cheery glow: soup, corned beef, and dehydrated potato. Though we were not exactly replete, at least we had enough to eat and were thankful for small mercies. Food was very scarce down at Camp 6, we gathered from Maurice, and they felt miserably deserted there – no porters left, and rice allocated as sparingly as if it was gold dust.

Camp 7 was indescribably dirty. The floor was a sea of mud and there was nowhere to cook except on the ground. Everything was wet; boots were like blotting paper which had been immersed in water, moisture covered the cameras and fungus grew on the lenses. The rain began at 4.30 p.m. and continued with an increasing ferocity. Torrents roared outside the shelter and smaller tributaries made their way inside so that the hammocks resembled white water canoes.

Mo didn't feel well so, after dosing himself with pills, he departed to his tent, clutching a copy of *Mountaineering Medicine*, his favourite book. The small bivouac tent was perched above the liquid mass of the swamp like a desert island. A few minutes later we heard a startled yell; a large spider had found its way into Mo's tent, obviously attracted by the only dry place in the vicinity. Joe, too, was feeling rough. The daily clearing of his throat, formerly a morning chore, now extended throughout the day; the end products of this protracted ritual resided in an empty tin of Jungle Nuts. This spittoon he deemed necessary, due to the lack of viscosity of his by-product!

I started to write the *Observer* report by the light of the lamp. I had arranged for a runner to take it out from Camp 6 the following morning; Mike and Maurice would take it on the first stage of the journey as they planned to go down to Camp 6 for food. The porters were expected to arrive there shortly. In my personal letter that night, to Jeremy Hunt of the *Observer*, I wrote:

El Dorado Swamp,
20 October

Dear Jeremy,

Things are a bit rough here: shortage of food and no helicopter lift. We also seem to have some sort of fever in camp – Mo has gone down with what looks like malaria (but don't mention this in the paper). Last week we discovered that about half the kitbags of food which were left at Camp 1, never reached Camp 6. We cached some food at Camp 4 for the trip out and some porters have been sent to collect this, for there are only three days' supplies left at Camp 6 and the situation is serious ...

After I had written the article I dashed out into the deluge, heading for my tent which stood on an adjacent islet to Mo's and had been constructed that day. I was soaked and mud-splattered by the time I threw myself into the tent.

'How are you doing, Mo?' I shouted.

'Not so good. Got a hell of a fever, as well as diarrhoea – have to go out every few minutes.'

'Anything I can do?' I volunteered.

'No thanks.'

The rain continued unabated until 8 a.m. I dreamt I was in a woodskin, shooting the rapids of the diamond waterfall and woke to hear new streams rushing past the tent and a retching noise from Mo's tent. I was concerned about him for he seemed in a bad way and the expedition might fold up without him.

Miraculously we had porridge without lumps that morning, and some hot reconstituted milk. Then Mike and Maurice set off, taking with them their rucksacks, my report, and some exposed films. Joe was still feeling ill and didn't emerge from his hammock. Don and I sorted out climbing gear for the face. We had decided to go up the next day, despite the fact that we hadn't any personal climbing equipment. Don had constructed a homemade climbing harness from nylon tape. It was ironic that the designer of the Whillan's harness was the only member of the expedition who didn't have, or couldn't borrow, one which would fit his ample girth. The four which Joe had supplied from his shop in Llanberis were all small sizes, more fitting for a lithesome girl than Don's forty-four-inch midriff! I packed up some personal oddments and enough foodstuffs for a couple of days at Camp 8, the camp in the cave at the bottom of the Prow.

It was a day of cloud, reminiscent of a November day on Rannoch Moor; thick, cold cloud, at saturation point, hung about like sphagnum moss and the Swamp appeared even more phantasmagorical than normal. I was standing by my tent when I spied two large birds circling to the left of the Prow. The sky had cleared momentarily. I guessed they must be Harpi eagles which were reputed to nest in the area. Schomburgk had seen Harpis in the 1800s, on the other side of Roraima. Don peered at them through his Zeiss binoculars, and he agreed they were big buggers all right, but not as big as the condors he'd met in Patagonia.

Mike was lucky, for he and Maurice arrived at Camp 6 to learn that Oswald, the porter, had just arrived with two of his fellow Amerindians with supplies from Camp 4. There was now a small amount of tea, coffee, sugar and rice. He also gathered that Bob Fernandez had been sent back to Georgetown by Adrian to collect more food, whilst Isaac Jerry was scouring the villages in an endeavour to find porters. Mike was alarmed at the despondency at Camp 6. Though the scientists were continuing with their collections, there was an air of depression throughout the camp; Jonathan and Maurice 'the Spy' were continually niggling like a couple of prima donnas. The advent of tea and coffee did much to cheer their spirits, though Neil still partook of the palm tea which he preferred. But relations were strained: the oft repeated refrain 'Morning has broken', was preying on Alex's mind, especially the second line which Neil invariably sang out of key. And Neil had heard from an Indian of a large capybara weighing 200 lb. and he constantly reminded Alex and Gordon that they must film it. This almost caused hypertension in the two technicians.

Mike and Maurice arrived back at Camp 7 at 5 p.m., sweating and drenched by the celestial watering can. They were heavily laden with climbing equipment and additional food supplies. In no time we had a brew going and ministered to our two invalids with steaming mugs. Mo had taken a dose of antibiotics earlier in the day but still felt like a lukewarm cadaver.

We all went to bed early as, once again, it was wet and miserable. I slept as sound as Rip van Winkle, but was up with the humming birds and into the shelter with alacrity for my daily porridge. Don and Mike had disembarked from their hammocks and Mike was busying himself, as usual, over the stove. He even made breakfast for Maurice (who was, theoretically, our cook!). Joe and Mo both felt as ill as ever, so Don and I shouted our farewells as, laden with heavy packs, we set off with Maurice to the bottom of the wall. We were to establish camp there and start climbing the following day.

I actually enjoyed the climb up the ridge. The trail seemed

easier now, or at least I accepted it as an ox dutifully accepts the treadmill. We recognized the landmarks: the first mud wall; the corridor of roots; the ridge of the bromeliads; the Gap and the Big Mud Wall; then the final steep climb up over roots and branches which had run amok, to the pool at the very bottom of the Prow. This would be the water supply for Camp 8.

It was good to reach the cave: a dry sanctuary. It had been formed by the dislodgement of large square blocks of sandstone, several fragments still remained on the ledge. The dust on the floor was dry; it was obviously a popular place for the legions of hairy spiders, scorpions and centipedes and I didn't relish the thought of sleeping on it that night, in the company of some aggressive spiders in red underpants. Earlier I had teased one with a stick while it stood its ground, displaying a fine set of fangs fashioned like a turner's exterior calipers. So I decided to put up my hammock.

It took us about four hours to clear the ledge and fix the tarpaulin to the edge of the overhang, to form a draped curtain which enclosed the cave. I balanced precariously, one foot on Don's shoulder, whilst I put in the necessary pegs for attachment. Farther along at the point where the climbing rope hung down. we tied the tent flysheet to make another smaller shelter. I slung my hammock under the big tarpaulin, suspended a good five feet from the floor of the ledge and, all things considered, it seemed quite snug. We made a brew, using a large sandstone block the size of a tea-chest, as a table.

'What are all these metal cigar tubes doing here?' asked Don, pointing to Joe's cigarette containers which were pigeon-holed in the cracks.

'Joe's menagerie,' I replied briefly, removing some dead bees from the bag of dirty brown sugar.

'There's enough of these crawlies about here without collecting them,' remarked my companion, throwing a handful down over the allotment. 'When you've seen one spider, you've seen them all.'

By the time we had sorted all the equipment out for the following day, rain clouds were advancing across the forest. The wind was stirring now and held that quality of rising power which indicates bad weather to come.

'What do you fancy for tucker, Don?'

He seldom did any cooking and as I have to eat (he seems able to go without), I had long since resigned myself to this chore. We decided on snake and pygmy and some soup, and while I got a brew up going Don went down to the pool to wash some of the filth off him. We certainly looked as if we had just knocked off from a pit face shift.

It started to rain and the wind tugged furiously at the tarpaulin ties, as if it was a mainsheet exposed to a storm, which couldn't be furled. I looked up at my handiwork on the overhang and regretted the space I had left between the sheet and the rock, rain was driving through the gap and running down on to my hammock. I ate my meal standing up, in considerable discomfort, for there were too many insects about and the tarpaulin slapped at my face like a gigantic yellow hand. Don returned with a partly filled can of water.

'You'd better doss in my wee shelter,' he advised as he wolfed down his steak and kidney pie before it became completely cold. He was clad in his waterproof suit, hood up and back to the foul weather.

I eyed the tiny space apprehensively and also the shoot leading from the unprotected cliff edge down over the bromeliads to the lip of the lower wall, and decided I would dash down to Camp 7 and come up at first light. Don, however, said he would get into the back of the ledge and hope not to get bitten in the night. Somebody would have to try and fix the tarpaulin a bit better next day. The boys could do it, if they came up. We would need all our energy for climbing.

I sang Kipling's 'Route Marching' as I went down:

'With the best foot first
And the road a-sliding past,
An' every blooming campin'-ground
Exactly like the last . . .'

relying on the theory (Mo's ingenious suggestion) that
snakes and other lethal beasties would find my singing so
distasteful that they would evacuate the area. I went as fast
as I could and managed to get to El Dorado swamp by the
time darkness was creeping across the forest like an insidious
tide of ink. It's impossible to rush in this type of country,
and too dangerous, one stumble and the unwary could be
impaled on a lance-like stake, or have an eye removed by a
branch severed at head height.

'Hello, Hamish, you're back soon.'

Mo was standing outside his tent, looking as white as a
blank sheet of foolscap.

'Bit stormy up there,' I replied, shaking myself, for I was
soaked to the skin. 'Going back up at first light.'

'Where's Don?'

'Oh, he's sticking it out in the far side of the overhang.
Got part of the tent up there, but there's not much room.
How are you feeling?'

'Bloody green, I can tell you. But I think the antibiotics
are having some effect now.'

I went over to the shelter where Joe was still in his hammock.

'How's "phlegm" Brown?'

'Oh, it's you – I thought we were going to get a rest from
the squeamish puns for a bit.'

Fortunately for me, my arrival coincided with the opening
of a tin of plums – their first goody for a week, as Joe pointed
out in mock anger. While we ate I learned that Alex and
Gordon had been up and got a bit of film. As soon as their
tripods and films arrived, they'd need to stay up here, but

they didn't seem to be looking forward to coming up. It was too cold and miserable.

Adrian was due back in a couple of days. The others were certainly short of food. They had been on five spoonfuls of rice per day, and little else. Neil would be going home looking as thin as a fer-de-lance at this rate.

At dawn I gulped down my porridge and set off up the trail to join Don, taking with me another Gaz cylinder. It was drizzling but looked as if it wouldn't be too bad a day. The others decided that they would try to get up to Camp 8 in order to repair the bivouac for us, as well as fixing a rope ladder on the nasty mud pitch which had so deteriorated that it was now impossible to climb without getting completely covered in black mud. I didn't see any snakes on my journey, but a friendly humming bird followed me for part of the way. I was feeling fit and made good time. Don was drinking a brew when I reached the bivouac.

'How do – you're up bright and early.'

'I've brought the Gaz,' I answered. 'Any tea left?'

'Aye, there's some in the dixy; I knew you'd be up if I made some.'

'The lads are coming up too ... going to make a rope ladder.'

'It's about time that was done; we won't get any other porters up, except Maurice, and the boys had to teach him to use jumars.'

I was by this time reclining on my rucksack, idly watching a centipede move up an adjacent rock.

'Have a good night?'

'Well, there were a few things crawling about, you know, but they seemed to settle down. I had to use my Message * a few times.'

'Hey, something's been eating the grub, look at this,' I held up a packet of sugar with a nibbled hole at the corner. It looked like a mouse, (though we didn't think there were

* The Whillans 'Whammer' – a multi-purpose piton hammer.

any up there. In future we would have to hang the kitbags from pegs – we couldn't afford to lose any more food.

Don had greatly perfected his makeshift harness earlier that morning and now clipped it on to the fixed rope with his jumars. In a few minutes, he was suspended out from the cave, but still held in check by the rope which was tied off beside his bivouac. He had a great view of the lower Diamond Falls, looking over to the watershed of the Paikwa.

Joe appeared round the corner of the face, closely followed by the others. I borrowed from Henry Lawson, whose verse seemed peculiarly apt for our expedition:

' "Who's that come amongst us?" asked the Leader of the Push. Cor strike me dead, it's bloody Fred, the Bastard from the Bush." '

'We've come to repair your house,' answered the master plumber with a grin.

'Good man – install hot and cold running women as well, would you?'

'Boy, I feel knackered,' he said.

'So does Mo,' I observed, for he was white-lipped and looked exhausted.

'We've brought up a plastic water carrier, Hamish, and some cord for lashing the tarpaulin,' said Mike.

'And we've got also a snake in this plastic bag,' added Joe, holding up his latest prize.

'Okay, Hamish.' Don was up the first pitch so I put the jumars on the rope and started to move up. I had a bird's-eye view of my friends busying themselves as they rehung the sheet. Joe was dangling from a peg under the overhang, one muddy foot descended on to my hammock.

'Hey, Brown, get your stinking foot off my bed! – I've got to sleep there tonight.'

'Oh, stop moaning, McInnes: it'll proof it – "nothing quite like it for cooling the blood!" '

I was feeling elated, despite the fact that my feet were being crushed in the nylon loops of the jumar for my cane cutter's boots were as flexible as sandshoes. I chanted the 'Mingulay Boat Song' merrily. Down below, Mo mimicked bagpipe drones derisively as he had a piss.

'Why do you whistle and sing off key, Hamish?'

'Much more difficult to do, you Welsh leek,' I retorted.

As I approached the top of this first fixed rope I noticed that it was already showing signs of fraying and was relieved that we now had another safety rope, running parallel to it. As I moved up on my two jumars, the safety jumar dragged up behind on the other rope. If, by any chance, the fixed rope should break, this lower jumar, connected by a short sling to my safety harness, would hold and I would only fall a couple of feet before it became taut. I looked up to the right and saw that Don had already started moving from the Niche. Above our heads, the Prow leaned out at a ridiculous angle. It seemed foolhardy to think that we could force a route up over these awe-inspiring overhangs, I told myself, but there was no alternative. If we had chosen a route closer to the Diamond Waterfall, where the rock was less steep but more broken, we would have risked drowning. We noted later that after heavy rain, vast quantities of water were blown straight across the face for about a hundred yards from the waterfall.

I stepped gingerly across the Niche, keeping a wary eye out for scorpions, and then shouted up to Don:

'Are you up yet?'

'A couple of minutes.'

'Okay.'

I clipped on and was soon swinging out over the crack which Joe had climbed. The rope he had fixed led directly up to the edge of the Cabbage Patch where there was an awkward thrutching move from the top of the rope past a large bromeliad, and on to the ledge. Don was over to my right, pausing on a section covered with exotic-looking plant-life.

'Well, this is where we start our shift,' he mused, looking up. 'Doesn't look too desperate for a bit, does it?'

I squinted upwards:

'Could be worse, I suppose. Depends on the wildlife though.'

Joe had left the climbing rope on the ledge for us, so we now sorted it out, plus various pegs and karabiner clips. Then we roped up. Don moved up a few feet, and came back down again.

'Seems okay,' he remarked nonchalantly, like a gourmet sampling a rare wine.

I took over the lead. Some way up were two ledges built into the corner immediately above the one we stood on. I led up on to the higher one, following a crack to my left in which I managed to anchor a bong and a peg. The corner itself had a good peg crack so I suggested that Don should join me in order to belay me. This would give me plenty of rope to try and gain yet another ledge – a tiny one – which was about ninety feet above. From that point, the corner seemed to sweep up unbroken for a further ninety feet until a terrace ran off towards the right. We were pinning our hopes on that terrace, as there seemed to be nowhere else to establish camp on the lower half of the face.

It had started to rain again, but it was dry and quite pleasant in our corner. At least, so I thought until I threw a loose stone off and uncovered a large brown scorpion. Once Don was belayed, I put in a peg and stood up on my etrier (a tape loop which acts as a stirrup when clipped on to a peg). I made reasonably fast progress, for the cracks were good, and saw only one more scorpion and a couple of spiders, one about five inches in breadth. In the back of the corner crack I noticed tiny nests, but couldn't tell if they were the homes of spiders or humming birds, since the owners were not in residence. I was lucky that there wasn't much vegetation in this corner, nothing like the quantity which Joe had met on the previous pitch, but a fine lichen, which my movement dislodged from the rock, got into my eyes and mouth – it felt as if I was following a caravan of mules along a dusty trail. I wished fervently I had the protective goggles, supplied by the Hilti company which were left at Camp 7.

'Can you keep into the corner, Don? There's a loose block here.'

'I can't get in any closer,' he shouted back.

I was now about eighty feet above him and had just reached a ledge about the size of a biscuit tin lid. It was actually the top of a loose block and not the best of possible stances, I reflected. Don was dressed in a waterproof suit and virtually nothing else and was feeling the cold. He had been stationary for over four hours. In my attempt to circumvent the block without knocking off too much loose material, a jammed nut came out and I fell on to a lower tied-off peg which fortunately offered adequate protection and I was none the worse. I threw the vegetation growing on the block out over Don's head, and it spiralled down to the foot of the crag. I was convinced that there must be nasties in this territory but, despite careful scrutiny, I found only one spider. Farther up the corner, the difficulties increased again. Between my outstretched legs, one on each side of the corner, I could look down to Camp 7 and the tiny splashes of vivid colour which betrayed the whereabouts of the lads, making their way back to camp. I could also see the site of Camp 6 in a clearing below the main escarpment. Although it was still raining 'outside', visibility was remarkably clear.

It was now getting on for four o'clock and not worth trying to do any more. We would have to use this stance to give us enough rope to reach the big vegetated terrace. I spat on the wall to try and get rid of the pollen-like dust. Half an hour later I had joined Don on his ledge, tired and bedraggled. My feet were killing me, crushed by the pressure of the etrier. I rubbed my right instep with a mucky paw. I also appeared to have broken my big toenail – probably when the nut pulled loose. We abseiled rapidly down to Camp 8, glad that we hadn't to go back to 7 that night; though we were filthy, it was at least reasonably dry filth, not the tenacious muck of the trail.

We had a good meal and enjoyed a particularly fine evening. We could see right across the rain forest towards Ayngdikes, which John Streetly had climbed, whilst, in the distance, smoke could be seen drifting up from the forest, probably Indians clearing bush for their cassava crops.

'Well over a hundred feet today, Don! We could run a lottery on it, like they do on board ship.'

'Aye, I wonder what odds the Georgetown bookies are giving us now?' replied Don, lighting a fag.

'Don't know. I fancy Cham gives hot tips on his Zero Delta!'

'Just think of the time it would take to walk through that forest,' marvelled Don pointing to the north-east where mile upon mile of undulating canopy stretched out.

Dusk was settling in by the time I climbed up into the back of the cave to get into my hammock. We no longer needed the mosquito nets, the atmosphere was too cold. I read *David Copperfield* for an hour by the light of my headlamp.

It was a cold clear night and we both slept well, though I heard a rustling during the night and shining my torch downwards I caught sight briefly of a small animal scuttling towards a hole opposite where Don was peacefully slumbering. We later discovered that it was a spiny rat, a rare creature; Mike Atherley and I both saw it more than once and thought that it had no tail. It was obviously partial to oatmeal and tuna fish, but Oxo cubes remained untouched. No doubt, this was the culprit responsible for pinching our sugar.

'I can eat this stuff all right,' said Don with relish next morning, tucking into a bowl of porridge. 'That quick-setting stuff – three quarter aggregate – that we got at Camp 7 would be the death of me.'

I had made it a bit thinner because I couldn't stand the

Blue Circle stuff, either. We would have had to swallow a stick of 'jelly' some day as an enema, if we'd kept on with that. My big toenail had come off overnight, and I found a nasty thorn in my finger. Even with the aid of the tweezers on Don's Swiss Army knife, I could not dislodge it.

We descended to Camp 7 at 10 a.m. The new rope ladder made the descent much easier and I was confident we'd now have no trouble in getting the Indians up to the face.

At Camp 7 we discovered that Mike and Maurice were proposing to go right down the trail and meet the porters, for the food shortage was now acute. Mike seemed to be completely inured to the long monotonous walks between camps and moved along the treacherous trails almost as fast as Maurice. Jonathan had come up to Camp 7 the previous day in two and a half hours. He was obviously pleased with his effort and Mike nobly forbore to tell him that we had done that same trip in two hours – with usefully filled rucksacks.

Maurice had been collecting insects in the slime forest and at El Dorado swamp for Mike Tamessar. He had the most amazing reactions, catching even the fastest-flying insects with ease. I was poking inexpertly at the thorn in my finger with a needle when he came over, and in an instant had quietly removed the offending article.

'I think I'll go and visit the Whillans recreation field,' I said, sucking the wound clean and exiting via the rear entrance of the shelter, snatching a piece of the fast disappearing toilet roll en route.

'I hope you're not going to make as much stink as you did up at Camp 8,' retaliated Don. 'I felt weak for hours afterwards.'

'I find bromeliad leaves on the face make excellent disposable bed-pans,' remarked Joe with a superior air. 'Just hurl them over on to the cabbage avalanche!'

Maurice and Mike set off. Little did we know it at the time, but this was the last we were to see of Mike until we were reunited in London, after the expedition. Joe went down to

Camp 6 later in the day to see if he could extract some food from Jonathan who was avariciously guarding the depleted kit bags. It was decided that Mo and Don should go back up to the face later that day. Joe hoped to return the following morning so he took his sleeping bag with him. We had more or less given up all hope of getting the helicopter at this late date, but there was a distinct possibility of an air drop. As this was our main hope, we didn't like to leave Camp 7 unattended. We had smoke canisters all ready, in case we heard a plane.

It was very quiet when everyone had left Camp 7. The birds became more inquisitive and a large butterfly, with vast fuselage, actually flew through the shelter. Maringma and Wei-Assipu were clear; their weird, contorted outlines looked like vertical pieces of a jig-saw puzzle. I lay on Don's hammock and read most of the day, for my insteps were painful. I heard a plane in the afternoon, but it was in the west. I managed to get a fire going, lighting it with the Gaz stove, and it was used thereafter throughout the expedition. In the evening I made myself a simple meal of soup and rice.

Next morning, Don's piercing whistle, like that of the twelve o'clock bee, echoed above me. I went out to see what was the matter, but he was only starting up the fixed rope; the whistle was to acknowledge a bright morning. I wandered round the swamp taking photographs. It never ceased to astound me, with its profusion of weird plants, mostly of the pineapple family. I realized that I was beginning to snuffle and hoped that I wasn't catching the El Dorado Swamp fever. Joe hadn't turned up by late afternoon and I became worried, wondering if I should go down to Camp 6. I decided that I ought to: Joe had gone down on his own and I had no means of knowing that he had reached the lower camp safely. I would have a difficult time explaining to his wife, Val, I reflected, if anything had happened. I could hear hammering on the crag, but during a lull, I shouted out what

I intended doing and after about ten minutes of abortive yelling, finally got the message across.

I set off smartly, carrying only an empty rucksack as I intended to return that night before dark. I went as fast as I dared down through the slime forest. I was beginning to feel weak and knew that I had caught the dreaded swamp lurgy. The temperature change as I went down was very noticeable. With each step, it grew hotter, I felt as if I was entering a steam laundry and by the time I reached Camp 6 the sweat was pouring off me, I was as soaked as if there'd been a cloudburst.

'Good afternoon, gents,' I moved quietly into the clearing where Neil was standing, clutching a dixy lid with which he had been passing the time prospecting for diamonds – like a latter day Lasserty.

'How do, blue. Long time no see.'

'Hiya, Neil – just came down to see if the oysters and *pâté de foie gras* had arrived.'

They hadn't, but the tripod and the autoload cameras had, and so had Joe, so I could stop worrying about the possibility of him having been eaten by Brown-eating spiders. But the others were still waiting for porters. Alex was looking exceedingly gaunt and emaciated and Gordon was beginning to look rather drawn and tense too. Joe showed me a large scorpion which Mike Tamessar had collected, picking it up by the sting and examining its underparts like a mechanic with a new Lamborghini up on a ramp, studying the latest technical innovations. When he dropped it in a jar in order to pour alcohol over it the scorpion, as predicted, committed *hara-kiri* first. It stung itself to death, once it realized there was no escape.

I gathered that some of the porters had arrived the day before with Alex's tripod and some camera equipment and that another group was expected at any moment. The arrival of Adrian and Isaac was also imminent. Over the past week, Gordon related, life at camp had settled into a regular pattern, dwindling food stocks being the focal point. They were so sickened by porridge that it was unanimously voted not to have any for breakfast on the morrow; even monotonous rice was better than that. A minor dust-up had occurred when Jonathan, with a well intentioned display of public-school spirit, had made the rice. He had accomplished the unforgivable sin – in the present company of Guyanese of Indian extraction – of allowing it to become soggy. For Maurice 'the Spy' it was the last straw. More practically, Ragu announced that in future he would cook the rice himself. Mike Atherley volunteered to share the chore. There were further minor clashes between Jonathan and Maurice; obviously tension was building up. The strain of the past few weeks, together with the lack of food, was beginning to stretch nerves to near breaking point. Don and I had experienced this before on Everest, where some members had become completely unbalanced due to the rigours of expedition life and the constant exposure to danger.

The advent of Adrian and Isaac, plus ten porters, later in the day, was like the relief of Mafeking. They had plenty of food with them; the Indians were carrying enormous loads in their warishis. Immediately the atmosphere in the camp became buoyant and free; as if a camp of heroin addicts had simultaneously received bumper doses after weeks of deprivation.

'Another six porters are on their way,' Adrian told us, leaning on his stick. 'They should be here tomorrow.'

He looked tired; his energy output over the past few days must have been phenomenal. Yet, an ardent collector to the last, he told me of a wonderful blue-green mushroom which he had found, unlike anything he had ever come across in all his travels. Infuriatingly, he had no camera with him as he had been travelling as light as possible. I don't think that Adrian entirely recovered from this forced march until after the expedition.

There was the excitement of mail for us, too, but as all our letters were either of a business or personal nature, we had no real news from the outside world. When we eventually got back out to Georgetown we were amazed at what had been happening. It was as if we had stepped off the time-wagon for a couple of months, like men locked up in prison with no outside contact. There was still no personal kit bag for Alex, so he had to continue wearing borrowed pullover, trousers and underpants. I joyfully unearthed my boiler suit from a rucksack:

'I'll be all right for descaling a boiler now, Joe!' I called out happily.

He was busy unwrapping a box of cigars, as reverently as if they were his family heirlooms.

'I'll be okay for a few days' smoke, too,' he added contentedly. 'Provided they're not snaffled by my friends.'

The day so far had been fair, though the bright morning had given way to the tide of water vapour which always seemed to rise with the progression of the morning, so that by midday, an English fog poured into every recess and stilt-rooted tree of the forest. Large drops of rain started to fall, which soon lengthened as though the drops behind sought to catch those in front in their panic to reach the ground. As quick as I could say 'splash', the ground was awash and the ditches which the boys had dug round the camp, after the fashion of early Dutch canals in the Colony, were soon brimming over. A great bladder of water accumulated in the fly-sheet and it took the combined efforts of Neil and Gordon to dislodge it, disgorging like a miniature Kaieteur over the side of the shelter.

It was evident that I couldn't return to Camp 7 that night. The day was already well advanced and I was quite weak from the swamp bug. I resolved to make a hammock so Ragu gave me a heavy camp-bed cover. I threaded ropes through the canvas tubes at each side and it made an excellent hammock. I borrowed a spare sleeping bag from Joe and found my own mosquito face mask in the kitbag which I had left in the camp, so I was well organized for a night in the comparative comfort of this warmer camp.

In camp, I observed piles of botanical specimens which Ragu had collected; some of them were already packed into plastic rubbish bins, labelled and addressed to Kew Gardens. They were to be sent back by the regular BOAC flight, Georgetown to London. But Ragu had no plant press, and wouldn't be likely to get one, due to its weight, since the only items now being brought in were those absolutely essential to our expedition. Mike Tamessar was also short of technical equipment which would seriously curtail his activity. But Adrian had brought as much as possible, including the dauntingly heavy cases with the bolt guns.

'Hello, Zero Delta; hello, Zero Delta,' Cham's voice could be heard in the background as we waited in the palm thatched hut for the evening meal of rice.

I discovered that everyone had caught the prospecting bug. There had been nothing else to do, so they used to go off with their dixy lids and wash the gravel in the small streams close by. Neil, who looked much fitter now and must have lost a stone in weight, told me that he had found a few interesting concentrates. Even if he found a fortune in gold and diamonds, however, the area was, of course, an Amerindian reserve and we wouldn't be permitted to exploit anything. At least it had kept their minds off the food crisis – though I now hoped that it was a thing of the past.

Meanwhile, Don and Mo had had an exciting day on the face. The weather had been kind to them. Mo describes how they climbed the top section of the Big Diedre:

In the morning we jumared up to the Cabbage Patch and I climbed up to the high point. At first the pegging was straightforward, but a bit loose, so I tended to use nuts. However, the top section was, to say the least, harrowing. I think I found it particularly bad because I had an alarming experience on a small ledge near the top of the Big Diedre. I was reaching into a crack – a crack which I couldn't see into – and trying to find the correct size of peg for it. I was standing on the top loop of my etrier, which meant that I was just in balance with my last peg at waist level; in other words, slightly top heavy. Suddenly a spider appeared, six inches from my face, a tarantula rearing up on its hind legs in its fighting stance, right in front of my bloody face! I jumped off my etrier and swung off the peg. Whilst hanging like that, I pulled out my hammer from the holster and twatted it one. The whole business upset me as I thought, 'They're going to be all over this bloody terrace above me.'

Getting on to Tarantula Terrace was hard for the rock changed on that last fifteen feet. It was shattered and stuck to the surface like loose lime on an old cottage wall. Two pegs came out when I tested them. In the end I said to myself, 'Oh shit, I'll just climb up the bromeliads!' This I did, and then belayed Don up.

Don had his share of excitement on his ascent. He was blissfully jumaring towards Tarantula Terrace – his thoughts, no doubt, far away in some well-stocked bar – when he realized that a scorpion, one of the unusual brown buggers, was climbing down the rope towards him. The gap was closing remarkably fast. With a quick flip of the Whillans Whammer, the offender was projected into space, which no doubt engendered in that particular scorpion a permanent distrust for those new-fangled nylon lianas which offered such convenient means of communication between the ledges.

Don and Mo found the sloughed skin of a snake on the Terrace. Their first reaction was one of disappointment, mainly because of the lack of water. They moved cautiously round to the right on this extremely exposed and profusely vegetated ledge; treacherous, as was everything else we had encountered on the trip; plants overhung the cliff so that it was almost impossible to estimate the true brink of the Terrace. They had hoped to climb a chimney which we had seen from Camp 7, but discovered it was a watercourse. Traversing back to the eastern end of the terrace, they found the only solution – a desperate one: a smooth sweep of rusty blank rock leading to huge roofs far above. This would require plenty of bolting. Having ascertained these unpalatable facts, they abseiled back down to Camp 8.

That evening, Adrian told me of his trip to Maiurapai. I recorded the conversation on tape:

I left Camp 6 on the Tuesday morning. The instant we saw that there was little hope of the helicopter, I decided that we should get back to Maiurapai as soon as possible to organize the equipment cached there. So Isaac and I set off to cut a trail to the Paikwa. We took with us three Indians. We made camp only one night – it was rather late before we made it. The following evening we reached Maiurapai, at about 6 p.m. It was over twenty-six miles of walking and we spent part of the first day cutting a trail from Camp 6 to the Paikwa; three miles of extremely rough going over boulders, in the forest; three miles of very tough country indeed. Early on the second day, we crossed the Paikwa, and then followed the true right bank down to the Maiurapai savannah. This was part of an old trail which I had made in 1956 and had renewed on the reconnaissance in April with John Streetly.

Arriving at Maiurapai, I discovered that there was no boat. Bob Fernandez' boat had gone up the Waruma and we had no notion of when it might return. It did not arrive on the Thursday. I realized now that something was wrong and that Renton, one of the Indians, had probably set off, having moored the boat at Camp 1.

At two o'clock in the morning, we sent off three Indians, paddling in a small dugout up the Waruma. They then walked up the trail, since the Waruma was in flood, and found the boat which they brought down with their dugout in tow. Paddling back to Maiurapai, they arrived at 2 p.m. We then went down to the mouth of the Arabara river and found that all the people living there had either gone fishing or hunting, in preparation for the Halleluya festival. And so we went back that evening without having succeeded in obtaining help.

Due to the very heavy rain, it was possible to ferry the equipment higher up the Paikwa than normal. When we had done this, Isaac and I set off for his village, arriving there at nightfall, and managed to recruit five more bearers. We left at about four o'clock in the morning and got back to Maiurapai at 10 a.m. on the Sunday morning. Immediately, we piled more baggage into the canoe and set off up the Paikwa, making two journeys in all. I came up on the evening trip, arriving at 6 p.m. As we were unable to persuade Phillip [the hunter who lives at Maiurapai] to improve the trail, we decided that we would cut across from the Paikwa to the Waruma, close to the site of Camp 3. We arrived there about two o'clock the next day, the trip taking in the region of five hours. We then walked up the established trail on the Waruma to Camp 4, where we spent last night, and this morning we came back up to Camp 6. We saw some wild pigs on the way, and the spoor of an adult jaguar.

It was an impressive narrative and not a journey I myself could imagine undertaking too readily at the age of sixty-one.

Etrier

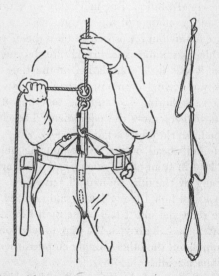

Abseiling with a Whillans harness and a figure of eight

Chapter 10

I am poured out like water, and all my bones are out of joint; my heart is like wax; it is melted in the midst of my bowels.

Psalm 22:14

I felt as lethargic as an old cow suffering from the staggers; my super-light canvas boots seemed to be anchored to the ground by an elastic rope: the El Dorado flu was triumphantly rampant. I dogged Joe's footsteps up the now familiar trail and dwelt upon the folly of this sort of life. Joe remarked that he had given up expeditions some time ago because they were so unpleasant; this trip only substantiated his early resolution. But inevitably, memories of the drudgery and monotony of ninety-nine per cent of expedition life are blunted in retrospect, and it is the more pleasant aspects which are remembered; such are the quirks of the mind. But it was little consolation at the time to realize that Alex was feeling even worse than me. He, Neil and Gordon were following Joe and me to Camp 8. We had six porters to help carry the equipment. The cloud hung low, as usual, but the day was fair.

Joe went on ahead of me. I was moving quite slowly, though I kept in front of the others, and at Camp 7 he had a brew going by the time we had all arrived.

'You look just how I feel, Alex,' I said ruefully.

'No,' he corrected me, 'I feel worse than I look.'

The porters had all arrived. We were to take four of them on to Camp 8, but the others simply emptied their warishis and set off back again.

Sipping a hot cup of powdered milk, Neil said he would

like to get a few shots of Joe and me leaving camp. I stood up, unfolding like a rusty engineer's rule. I doubted if I'd make it to 8 – I'd have to lighten my pack.

The weather was clearing as we moved up through the undergrowth above El Dorado Swamp. We heard hammering high up the face; the boys were hard at work. That morning Mo and Don had gone back up to Tarantula Terrace, fixing the ropes more securely. When they arrived at the Terrace, they drilled holes under an overhang for bolts which we could use to suspend two hammocks. This small overhang – like that at Camp 8 – would provide some shelter in this exposed position when a flysheet was draped over it. Mo tackled the section above the Terrace; a smooth blank red wall. When Don descended to Camp 8, he continued work for several hours, belaying himself on a thin 9 mm. rope whilst he stood in his etriers, drilling the bolt holes. On the first forty feet he had snapped four heads off the bolts and began to wonder if we would run short of them before we had completed the climb.

Joe and I arrived at Camp 8 with the four Indians and, just a few minutes later, Don dropped in – literally – like a well-fed spider returning to its den.

'How do,' he called cheerfully as he spun round above us.

The Indians looked up with awe. They were obviously fascinated by these rope techniques; I felt sure that, given the chance, some of them would be following us up the face. Already Maurice had indicated his interest. They should make superb, natural climbers with their precise judgement and physical prowess.

'Got any grub?' Don demanded as he was guided into the ledge by the tied-off end of the rope from his suspension point above the allotment.

'Yes, we're well stocked now, lad,' I assured him. 'Even got the personal climbing gear.'

'What's the Terrace like?' asked Joe, unpacking his Joe Brown Expendable rucksack.

'Plenty of room,' drawled Don. 'Looks hard above.'

I was emptying one of the kit bags which was hanging from a peg above the ledge when my hand encountered a spider. This was a constant war, the survival of the quickest, and I bashed it unregretfully with a tin of tuna fish.

An hour or so later we obtained a fine view of Mo's striped longjohns as he came towards us, arse first, on the last abseil.

'Don't fall out of your hammock tonight,' he warned. 'I'll be directly below.'

'So I see,' I returned drily. There was about six inches clearance between the two hammocks. 'It's going to be awkward when I have a piss!'

'Use a tin,' he advised. 'And make sure you don't spill it.'

'I wouldn't do a thing like that to my friends,' I mocked.

'I suppose we two will sleep in the tent bivvy, Joe?' Don queried.

'Yes, we'll toss up for who gets the outside berth. Are there many creepies about?'

'Not too bad,' replied Don. 'They seem to bugger off when they know we're in residence.'

'That spiny rat, or whatever it is, still does its nightly rounds,' Mo said. 'It has a nibble at most things.'

We had a pleasant night and the dawn was fine. It was a majestic sight to wake up at the base of the Wall and see the magnificent waterfalls leaping down to the Paikwa watershed. They seemed the epitome of the Lost World. With the exception of a few trails, made by pioneers like Adrian and Isaac, this northern area was totally unexplored. Its inaccessibility made me feel very insignificant and vulnerable; here the law of the jungle was predominant and we had to rely on a spasmodic dribble of supplies: if these were cut off, we should have to hot-foot it ignominiously back to civilization. It seemed that the spiders and scorpions realized this, tolerating our invasion in the knowledge that mere humans could only survive a limited time in their hostile environment. The place was alien as well as fascinating, it possessed a love-hate attraction. I felt we had been privileged to visit this hidden corner of the world, if only for a short time, but it was a frightening Paradise Lost. I felt under continual pressure – always on the alert. I remembered the words of Charles Waterton, describing his early home in the jungles of Guyana:

> 'Tis now the vampire's bleak abode,
> 'Tis now the apartment of the toad;
> 'Tis here the painful Chegoe feeds,
> 'Tis here the dire Labarri breeds,
> Concealed in ruins, moss, and weeds.

At 6.30 a.m. the next morning the three BBC men left Camp 7. Their destination was our camp; their purpose to film us; the human drama. Foolishly, they tried to carry too much. Neil, particularly had a hard time climbing the rope ladder pitch with a heavy rucksack and arrived exhausted at Camp 8. Alex, too, was worn out, drenched with sweat and looking as if he had been keel-hauled. Gordon seemed his normal self, but his face denoted the strain which lurked beneath the surface. We offered them an energy-restoring brew when they arrived.

I was languishing in my hammock, destined to remain there most of the day on account of the lurgy. Alex did some filming as Joe and Mo jumared up the fixed rope; they planned to stay on Tarantula Terrace for the night, so Don was going part of the way with them to haul equipment. My back was beginning to feel sore – just as Joe's had done with the El Dorado bug – so I resolved to stay the night there with Don in his small bivvy. At least I could lie stretched out, I thought hopefully. It would be a change from my hammock.

Some time later, the fresh face of Oswald came into view

round the bottom of the Wall. He had climbed up into the cave to join us, bearing a note from Mike.

'Hey, this is bad news, blue!' said Neil aghast. Mike was out of action. He had put a spike of wood through his foot and had had to be flown out to hospital. It happened down on the trail between the Waruma and the Paikwa. With the utmost difficulty, Maurice the Indian had helped him to reach a canoe on the Paikwa. That night, whilst he lay in his hammock, soldier ants must have picked up the scent of blood on his foot and marched into camp. Most of our hammocks had suffered from the rigours of the bush, and Mike's was no exception. The soldiers found a hole through which to breach his defence and climbed along the supports of the hammock. He awoke at the first bite – which stabbed like a hot needle – and shouted in alarm to the faithful Maurice. Maurice stirred the fire into life and, wielding flaming brands, diverted the ants away from Mike. One column, however, continued to invade the camp and emptied a kit bag containing thirty packets of noodles in record time. They had to wait at the Paikwa river camp for a couple of days, until a canoe could pick them up. Then, after a painful evacuation, Mike was eventually flown to Georgetown from Kamarang by the GDF. On his discharge from hospital he was flown back to the United Kingdom.

The loss of Mike from the expedition was a stunning blow. Typically, he had received his injury while trying to ease our food shortage by again making that exacting trek through the rain forest. He was a supremely unselfish person to have on a trip.

Don started climbing and I crept out of my hammock, like a centenarian roused from his deathbed, to launch the haul bag once he had reached the top of the first pitch. The others had returned to the Swamp so I was on my own. I watched the blue Karrimor sack disappear above, then gazed out over the forest. The weather was improving; each day the periods of sunshine seemed longer. Here at Camp 8, life was quite comfortable – the most pleasant camp on the whole march. The prodigious mass of Roraima seemed to function like a heat storage tank. The sun's rays warmed the mesa enough during the day for it to act as an enormous 'hot brick' for our comfort overnight. (This was only true when there was no cold water running down; we discovered higher up, that it was extremely wet and unpleasant.)

I had a good meal going by the time Don dropped in. It was a superb evening with the sun's rays streaking across the forest in golden shafts. The distant savannah, which we could see over the watershed between Wei-Assipu and Maringma, looked inviting. Free of trees, it would be a pleasure to walk there, I thought, without stumbling over roots, clutching a cutlass or snake stick. I enjoyed that evening with Don. We sat on kit bags on the ledge, on the alert for stray scorpions. I had already crushed one with my boot while I was making the meal.

Though it had been a fine evening, it was a wild night. It rained cats and dogs, the deluge battering against the thin flysheet, and the wind howling like a coyote. Once I awoke, panic-stricken. I was convinced there was a snake inside my bag – but it was only Don's foot; we were lying head to toe on the narrow ledge and he was twitching in his sleep. Later, I heard a rustling and the noise of two Gaz cylinders being knocked together. I flashed my torch, which was always ready for nocturnal investigations (a necessary precaution in the Guyana forests) and caught a glimpse of our pal, the spiny rat. It was scuttling between Don and the flysheet.

'Hey, Don, get that rat!'

I have seldom seen Don perturbed, but he leapt up then and whipped his sleeping bag down in a single swift movement, shamelessly revealing his birthday suit.

'The bloody thing's in my bag,' he cursed in alarm. I don't think it was, actually, but the space between the flysheet and Don was extremely small so the rat must have seemed un-nervingly close as it wound its way down between one of

England's best-known mountaineers and the thin layer of bri-nylon which constituted the flysheet. Later, when Mike Atherley stayed at the camp, he tried to shoot the rat with his automatic, but I am happy to report that he was unsuccessful. Despite its thieving tendencies, it was one creature which was not well-endowed with weapons, and it left us unmolested. Besides, it gave the place a feeling of home; nothing like a friendly rodent to make one feel established!

I was quite dry that night as I had the rear berth; though it was more vulnerable as regards creepies, it had the advantage of being sheltered. Don's sleeping bag was saturated by morning. I was feeling better but decided to spend the day in bed; with luck I would soon be fully operative again. It was important that I should get some film of the route for, as yet, we had no coverage whatsoever of the climb; and we were already one third of the way up.

Don returned to El Dorado swamp to collect some dry gear and rope. He found Alex lying in his sleeping bag, almost ready to receive the last rites. The previous evening he had dosed himself with Codeines to try to stop his uncontrollable shivering.

Later, Mo and Joe came down and I prepared a meal for them. They were tired and filthy. They had continued the climb the day before, from Tarantula Terrace. They perked up over the meal and began to relate their recent activities. Mo had spent some time on his own, bolting above the Terrace. The first bit was about thirty feet, then the Wall dipped back a bit so that he couldn't see any more from the Terrace. But, up above, cracks started to appear and continue.

It took him most of the day to put a couple of bolts in, with some weird tie-off pegging to do. It was all uphill stuff, and it took a long time to reach the foot of an expanding flake. Mo hadn't liked it at all. He climbed it on nuts – nuts in opposition to concentrate the load in the right direction.

'Even the Baron here didn't fancy it – that pleased me no end!' he pointed a triumphant finger at Joe.

'What's this Africa Flake?' I asked, for it had been mentioned before and was difficult to see from below, even with binoculars. 'Nothing even remotely resembles an outline of Africa on the face.'

'It's like a map of Africa if you were looking at it from underneath,' Mo elucidated.

'Typical Welsh reasoning that,' I replied in disgust.

Joe was belayed down on Tarantula Terrace for a lot of the time, enjoying himself for the first time in ages in the sun. This morning, they had gone up to Mo's high point again, and Joe led up about fifteen feet with three pegs, but he was a bit nervous about hammering them into the edge of the continuation of the flake which was so thin it looked as if it might snap off. He climbed about forty feet round the first overhang, just using jammed nuts and hand jams. But then, there was nowhere to fix nuts; it was absolutely unavoidable to use pegs, which took a couple of hours. Apart from the physical effort, he was gripped. The thought of bashing a peg in and prising off that huge overhang was unthinkable, so he descended.

As all their gear was above, Mo and Joe were going back up for the night. Joe's chief concern was for his cigars. He had opened several tubes and they were all covered in fungi. I hoped it was a culture good for his lungs. I promised, however, to come up in the morning to do some filming at the Africa Flake. Already I was feeling a lot better, so promised to be at Tarantula Terrace at about nine o'clock in the morning.

Mo clipped his jumars on to the rope and started to move rhythmically upwards, like a puppet soldier marking time. Joe followed him. But they had left it rather late and were forced to climb the last hundred feet to the Terrace in total darkness.

The following day was a Sunday. I was up before dawn. The cloud was spread out in front of me so that only the proud tops of the neighbouring mesas stood out above the swirling clouds, as they must have appeared in past eras, rising from the sea.

I put the cine camera into a kit bag and tied it to my climbing harness so that it would hang about six feet below me as I ascended. I stepped regretfully over the red Hilti bolt gun container. It had been brought to camp – all the way from Maiurapai – only to discover that it wouldn't work. The rock of Roraima was so hard that even this superb tool was unable to fire bolts into the thin cracks.

I felt weak and tired, but made remarkably good progress. Mo was still in his hammock when I eventually arrived at Tarantula Terrace. The Terrace was fascinating, though the fact that the toilet was situated close to the entry point of the sanctuary detracted from my first impressions. A large bromeliad had been the chosen recipient and fulfilled the function of a living cesspool. No doubt, the plant was astonished by this manna from heaven, but nevertheless it succeeded admirably in sustaining the appalling smell for the duration of our stay on the face!

'You blokes still in your pits?' I gasped as I moved my jumars up the last stretch of rope which was covered in soil from the ledge. This always proved an awkward move, I was to discover.

'Joe does all the cooking from his hammock,' Mo explained. 'But one of these days he'll knock the stove off, right on top of me.'

One hammock was strung directly beneath the other, and Joe's cook shelf was a ledge about three inches square, situated at his hammock level. Balanced precariously on it was a steaming billy.

'Hey, Hamish,' said Joe. 'Get me some more water and I'll make another brew. You just milk those bromeliads over there,' he added instructively, pointing to where the great plants formed a wall on the edge of the Terrace. 'We've got used to the worms inside them now, although we'll probably all die a horrible death soon enough!'

I put down my kit bag and held a dixie under each large receptacle in turn, bending it over as if forcing a punchbag down on to the floor, to fill the pot.

'There's a hell of a stink here,' I complained, when I had returned from this precipitous errand. 'I thought you delivered your offerings to the gods on leaves, Joe?'

'The trouble is that from here, Hamish, it might land in Camp 8, where I don't think it would be well received!'

'Hey, watch it, Brown,' Mo looked upwards in alarm.

'Ah, dinna be bothered, laddie,' said Joe, using an empty curry bean tin for a minor call of nature, with more than his usual stealth – since I was filming him! Presently the container arced through space like a comet, with a tail of uric acid. Joe was smoking a cigar, having recovered from his early morning coughing spree. Mo was similarly enveloped in a cloud of Rothman's smoke.

It was about 9.15 before Mo started up the fixed rope leading to Africa Flake. There were two ropes already in place, both tied in at Tarantula Terrace, since otherwise they would have hung about twenty feet away from the Wall. The pitch was about 150 feet so it took a considerable time for both Mo and Joe to get established at the Flake. Meanwhile I had become rather bored and was feeling in need of more sustenance as I had had little time for breakfast at Camp 8. I decided to have some soup, so I climbed cautiously down the sloping Terrace to the large bromeliads, where I filled a dixie. Besides the usual stock of worms, an empty tin was lodged amongst the sword-blade shaped leaves. An hour later, well fortified by the soup, I had reached Joe who was standing in etrier from a peg on the Flake. As a situation, it was sensational; the Wall fell away below our feet to the rain forest. There was only one foothold on the Flake; Joe generously left this vacant for me. Mo had taken over the lead and was now in an almost horizontal position at full stretch, trying to put a peg in a crack in the wafer-thin flake.

'Some nice filming to do here, Joe,' I commented, pulling

up my kit bag containing the cine camera.

'Hey, Hamish,' shouted Mo from above. 'Did you get water from that bromeliad with the tin inside it?'

'Yes, I had a fine repast; chicken with vegetable stock.'

'Aye, Jock, you had more than bromeliad stock in that soup – that was Brown's piss tin that landed in that bromeliad . . .'

Joe gave his long, low cackle which resembled the noise made by a stick being run along railings.

I was suddenly aware of a bad taste in my mouth.

Mo later described his reactions to that superb pitch on the Africa Flake:

I hadn't done much pegging before, but I was learning all the time. It was a fantastic pitch; up right first of all, until I was out of sight of Hamish and Joe, and then back left again, above the Great Roof. I was climbing on tie-offs, mainly thin knife blade pegs partway in [small loops of tape employed close to the rock, on the body of the peg, to reduce leverage]. I had no qualms about them as, although the blades didn't go in far, I knew they were smashing.

I yelled down to Joe, 'Hey, Joe, I've got a hell of a lot of rope drag: it's desperate. I've almost reached a stance and I can't drag the climbing rope any more, so I'll untie and climb up on just the sack-haul rope.' I slipped the thin rope through a peg and then made about three peg moves, not clipping into anything. I was just moving up on a peg when it flirted out. I could have gone a real pisser but, as I dropped, I caught the edge of the rock with my hands and heaved myself up. If I hadn't managed to hold on, I'd have fallen fifty feet and found myself hanging over the Great Roof, way out from the face.

Meanwhile, I had climbed down to Tarantula Terrace and then continued on down to Camp 8, leaving the cine camera and some unexposed film stock in waterproof bags under the overhang. Neil and his companions were all at Camp 8 with Don. I reassured Neil that I'd got some climbing film at last and described progress above – smelly but interesting. I told them how Mo and Joe had got a sheet of plastic to catch the drips from the Bottomless Chimney, but it wasn't very successful and we were having to milk the bromeliads which was unpleasant, to put it mildly. My memory pricked uncomfortably.

In return Don told me the good news that we were getting an airdrop of about 150 lb. of food. Chan-A-Sue would be dropping it at El Dorado Swamp in the morning.

I had been able to see Alex's film tent from above. It was on the narrow section of the ridge, before the turn off to the Diamond Waterfall, and gave a terrific view of the face, though they had had a bit of a job putting it there. Alex was rubbing his Eclair with a clean section of cloth. He cared for his camera with an almost pathological intensity which was fully justified as he succeeded in making a superb film with a camera (the Eclair) renowned for its dislike of rough handling and wet conditions.

'You blighters should be down there now,' Don addressed Neil belligerently. 'A great day for filming, and you're all farting about here!'

The stuff I had taken up on the Flake ought to be good, but we would need other material for editing and it was not often as clear as this. But Neil was unconcerned and wanted to film hands – hands doing things, Neil explained when we all looked blank. 'Close ups of hands . . .'

'You know, Neil, we had all sorts of smart BBC buggers on the International Everest trip. They made me bloody sick. You should be down in your shelter filming the lads up there,' he pointed up the Wall. 'That's what it's all about. You'll get yourself and the other lads here exhausted if you come up to Camp 8 every day, like the Grand Old Duke of York.'

This was the uncompromising beginning of an ever widening rift between Don and Neil. 'Go to hell,' said Neil amicably.

But Neil is a professional film-maker and it was obvious to

me later that he was right, for the film which Alex took at the bivvy was some of the best of the expedition.

Meanwhile, as Don cut the fingertips out of a pair of industrial rubber gloves in order to let the water out, I heard the latest gossip from the lads. Some of the others were moving up to stay at Camp 7. Jonathan and Maurice 'the Spy' had continued their mutual hate campaign. Ragu and Adrian had already sent plant specimens back via the Indian porters, for shipment to Kew by BOAC.

Plants and clods of earth kept flying down from above, but they landed well out from the face amidst the allotment. Joe had started to climb up to Mo's stance above the Great Roof. We heard all about it later. Joe began the tale:

Mo disappeared out of sight just about the time you went down, then reappeared directly above me. It was really spectacular, and as exposed a pitch as you could imagine. Previously we had climbed by jumaring up one rope fixed at the top stance, while the last man was belayed on the other. On a straight pitch this system worked well. But not on this one. There were so many traverses that, when I attempted to use this technique, I found that I couldn't stay on jumars very easily and had to climb using the etrier. This involved a lot of really strenuous moves so, by the time I reached Mo, I was feeling pretty tired. Mo volunteered to continue, so I belayed him. It looked easy, but by the time he had climbed twenty feet it was obvious that the angle hadn't eased at all and he seemed to be leaning out. The rope was hanging free about six or eight feet away from the rock.

Mo took up the story next:

There was a fantastic traverse out left on a really great crack – brilliant pegs, one and a half inch angles, driven in about three inches. It then seemed to be comparatively easy ground, but I had run out of pegs which would fit the crack, so I retreated to Joe.

They accomplished for the first time ever, that terrifying abseil over the Great Roof. The first occasion was probably the worst as the rope wasn't hanging in the very best line for the descent. As Mo said:

We were thirty feet away from the rock on that horrifying abseil. It was the first one I had done so far away from the rock. The old arse was winking as I left but Joe had gone first and I wasn't too worried, really.

That night the two of them stayed at Tarantula Terrace. Four hundred feet below, Don and I just hoped the airdrop would happen as planned.

The preceding day we asked Neil to send up more rope with one of the Indians, but we had finished breakfast and there was still no sign of anyone coming up the trail. The morning was still so we tried shouting:

'Neil, Neil . . .'

Don's piercing whistle finally brought them out of the shelter at Camp 7. Irrepressibly, Lawson's 'Bastard of the Bush' sprang to my mind:

He scowled towards the north and he scowled towards the south
Then crooked his little finger in the corner of his mouth
And with a long, low whistle woke the echoes of The Rocks',
And a dozen ghouls came sloping round the corner of the blocks.

'Bring up the rope,' I yelled lustily.

A short time later, a small figure, burdened with a Gargantuan load, left El Dorado Swamp; it was Oswald. He reached us an hour later and we unloaded 650 feet of rope, for fixing up the face from his warishi. The walkie-talkies had arrived by porter, but we still had no means of communication with the two men on Tarantula Terrace. I had carried one walkie-talkie up with me when I went filming, but it flatly refused to function. Gordon promised a replacement so that we could establish a direct link from the Terrace down to Camp 7, which would avoid a lot of confusion. We had also planned to use the walkie-talkie for conversation in the film, but now realized that the battery was too shortlived for lengthy conversation.

Today was 29 October and Mo and Joe were both tired and stiff after the previous day's efforts, so they decided to have an off day. Joe was suffering from harness chafing, he had spent so much time hanging from pegs with his weight on the harness, that it had rubbed his skin raw. Later in the morning they descended to us for the much-needed rope. Joe arrived with a cigar box and a fistful of cigar tubes which he produced from his anorak pocket. More for the menagerie.

'Some fantastic insects up there,' he enthused. 'Wait till you see the latest bug from up on the face, it's got telescopic antennae!'

'These fancy creepy-crawlies will be the death of you, Brown,' Don warned. 'Why can't you leave the poor things in peace?'

Mo came into view just then from above, as Maurice Barrow and Mike Atherley arrived from below.

'Hello there, man,' Maurice shouted, somewhat out of breath.

He was bathed in sweat, though it could have been moisture from the thick cloud which had descended during the past ten minutes. Mike Atherley raised his hand in a deliberate salute. He looked the same as ever: an efficient soldier, not given to complaining – a man to take along.

'Let's weigh up job,' suggested Don pointedly.

We were right out of soup and meat, but with the new rope Oswald had brought we ought to be able to make a push for the next bivvy ledge above the chimney, well christened the Green Tower. The next section didn't look too bad, according to Mo, though we'd been known to be wrong. So he and I would wait for the next morning's airdrop and join Mo and Joe with some food and extra rope. Meanwhile, they would go on ahead today and take a couple of plastic water containers.

'Well, if that's settled, let's have something to eat,' suggested Don. 'Who's good at cooking?'

After Oswald had made a meal, Joe and Mo prepared to ascend to Tarantula Terrace. Oswald had filled two water containers, each weighing about twenty lb. Mo set off until he reached the Niche, from where he hauled up a kitbag of equipment. Joe then followed, trailing two hundred feet of rope behind him, the water containers attached to its end. When he got to the Niche, we helped to guide them up with a rear rope, in case they fouled on the overhang.

The dense cloud prevented the plane from making the scheduled drop until 5.30 p.m. During one of the infrequent clear spells, the yellow Islander swung into view, skimming the forest canopy. It seemed as if it must crash on the ridge beneath us, but it veered abruptly as it reached El Dorado Swamp and dropped down into the watershed of the Waruma, where an almost 2,000 foot escarpment plunged into the basin. A small package had been dropped. From our bird's eye vantage point, it appeared to fall over the edge. We learned later that it was a trial package to give the pilot his range. During the next few runs the drop was confined within a circle forty feet in diameter, which Cham had made. All the packages landed safely in this area before the cloud once again wrapped itself round the ridge and the note of the Islander faded as Chan-A-Sue circled at height, patiently awaiting another chance to swoop down towards the Swamp. But fuel was running short and he was forced to slant back to Kamarang.

Though we were still short of food, that air drop was a great mental boost. We now felt that we had a direct link with the outside world again. A moment before, we had been alone, on a limb, remote from civilization; even the Georgetown bookies were giving heavy odds against us. However, within an hour the food was being transported up to our camp by the Indians.

We started off at first light, hauling up food in kit bags and more water. We had one hundred feet length of corlene and, as Mo had suggested, tried to haul it up to Tarantula Terrace in one long pull. This proved unsuccessful and we had a frustrating and exhausting time, freeing it each time it snagged. I arrived first at the Terrace and was surprised to see that Joe had already started although it was only 9.15 a.m. I was disappointed as I was now unable to take the film sequence which I had planned. They had decided to try and make a push for the Green Tower that day and Mo was busy tying the end of a haul rope to a large rucksack, packed with their equipment. As Don arrived over the edge, Mo had begun climbing and the haul bag was swinging on the end of a rope, far out from the Wall, as Joe pulled it up to the Africa Flake.

Wearily, I hauled the bags up the last section of the Big Diedre, where they jammed once again, so I had to descend to free them. When I returned we made use of a simple winching system which employed the jumars.

'Wouldn't like to do this every day for a crust, Don.'

'Not likely,' he puffed and straightened up stiffly. 'What a bleeding weight!'

We discovered to our dismay that the water container had worn through in one section, due to the abrasion on the rock, and so we had only one gallon left of the original four. In about an hour we had sorted out the food and equipment and decided to follow round the Terrace to see if we could find a bivouac site on the other side of the Prow. Tarantula Terrace actually curved round the profile of the Prow and we thought the north-west side might be more sheltered.

Above we could see Joe jumaring up that frightening roof, his anorak billowing out so that he resembled an orange bat. Mo had reached the stance just below their highest point. The haul sack was hanging way out from the face, like a mason's plumb. Above it, the sky was a brilliant, electric blue; one of the finest days we had seen.

Mo describes the day's climbing:

I finished the pitch off, for I had the right pegs now, and it proved to be a lot harder than I had bargained for. There were plenty of spiders so getting on to the next stance was quite an effort. I got Joe up and we sorted out the ropes, as they were getting in a mess. I knew that we weren't going to get up to the Green Tower that day, even though we had got the bag up, but I traversed out to the chimney which we had seen from below, leading up to the Green Tower. Don had suggested that we should climb directly up from the last stance, but I didn't fancy that, although it looked drier. Anyhow, the chimney I was heading for had looked easy from below. By moving right I reached a position where I could look into it; it looked straightforward enough. There wasn't too much water coming down. Just as I was turning back to join Joe for the abseil back to Tarantula Terrace – it was now quite plain that we couldn't get up that day – I saw a bloody great worm: about two feet long, and purple! I was soaked to the skin because, above the Great Roof, we were exposed to drips and rain. It hadn't rained much but there were enough drips from the rock to ensure that we were both saturated. I abseiled down to Joe and we both went down the Great Roof, back to the Terrace.

The pits where Don and I chose to sleep lacked certain creature comforts (though not creatures) but were the best we could manage. Using a bolt at one end, and a piton at the other, I had slung my hammock under a large overhang, about one hundred precarious feet from the other refuge. Don hadn't bothered to take his hammock with him and proposed to sleep on the Terrace, just beyond me, where the ledge dipped and then ran level for a few feet.

It was just as well we had found other quarters, but we were informed in advance of the return of our friends and I was able to film them coming down. All sense of the vertical was lost on the climb; in the first instance one kept contact with it through the pitons, but once the fixed rope was in place the only contact with the rock was at anchor points. I fielded the haul bag on to the ledge; it had been clipped on to the abseil rope for lowering so that it was guided towards the Terrace. Joe followed it down.

'No go?' I asked.

'No, but Mo says the Bottomless Chimney doesn't look too bad,' he answered briefly.

He was descending slowly so that his figure-of-eight descendeur wouldn't heat up too much. It was a constant worry that they would overheat on descent, melting the nylon rope. Joe had already evolved the ingenious and successful technique of cooling them, at each stance on descent, in the water of the bromeliads.

As the other two reslung their hammocks, I made a meal and we discussed tactics. It was resolved that we should make an all-out effort to reach the Green Tower the next day, Don and I backing-up the other two. We planned to take two large haul bags and enough equipment to reach the summit; we had sufficient food for a further five days. I had cut the faulty water container in half and placed the sections in two bromeliads to catch water, a ruse which was proving successful.

The ledge at Tarantula Terrace was about two feet wide, the bromeliads forming a low fence, since their tops just reached above the level of the ledge from the steeply angled slope below. This slope merged into an overhanging wall which fell directly to the base of the Prow. All our belongings were hanging from pitons on the wall behind us. To our right, as we looked out over the forest, was the top of the fixed rope from the Big Diedre; immediately above it, twin ropes hung out free in a loop from Africa Flake. During the day I had fixed a handrail round the corner to our latest bivouac sites since the Terrace dipped down treacherously. After a meal, Don followed it along to his clearing in the shrubbery.

'Rather you than me,' I commented as he set off. 'I think you'll need a puncture repair outfit tonight!'

I followed later, by which time it was dark and I had to use my headlamp; one couldn't afford to put a single foot wrong. Don was already in his sleeping bag, making himself a pillow by the light of his lamp. There didn't seem to be too much livestock abroad, he said. But it was a bit early to tell – the late shift wouldn't have started yet.

It was an overcast evening. The cloud clung to the top edge of the overhang like grey wallpaper. I eased myself into my hammock, fully expecting the piton to fly out, though, as a further precaution, I had tied myself above the waist to another one. But all was well; I relaxed, pulling the flysheet of the spare tent round me to form a protective wall against the damp mist. In the light of my headlamp I could see ripple marks on the underside of the rock above me, as uniform as a sheet of corrugated iron. I shone the torch below me and caught a glimpse of a snake as it scurried under a heather-like plant which was growing on the ledge.

'You okay, Don?' I called anxiously.

'Aye, not bad.'

'I saw a snake just now.'

'Got you, you blighter . . . And you!'

The thuds of Don's Whammer could be felt vibrating within the rock. He was having a tough battle with the beasties.

I was most impressed with Tarantula Terrace. My hammock position was particularly fine; it reminded me of the Hall of the Mountain King. When I awoke, in the morning, the mists were clearing and a fresh wind was blowing over from Venezuela. The deep-throated roar of the waterfalls denoted that it had been a wet night, but we had been well sheltered. Don informed me that he had had a good sleep, after the initial influx of the nasties, and had remained dry. It was chilly and exposed to the cold wind when we joined the others for breakfast. They remained in their hammocks during this operation, as Joe was cook on the 'upper floor'.

We packed the haul bags for what we imagined would be the final assault on the Wall.

Soon we were jumaring up the fixed ropes, one at a time, with Mo and Joe in the lead. Don and I were to act as a support group, hauling the sacks up. I remained in the rear, filming the whole operation. I now had one of the autoload cameras which made my task easier, since they are magazine cameras. As soon as a magazine was exposed, it could be replaced immediately with a loaded one – no fiddly business of threading film over sprockets. We carried a walkie-talkie which was in good working order.

Don hauled the sacks up to Africa Flake and I jumared up to join him. I was alarmed to find that the section of rope immediately below the anchor piton had been badly worn and was in a dangerous condition. We hauled in enough slack to allow the damaged bit to be taken in, above the peg.

Don carried on above, first moving out horizontally from Africa Flake, having clipped on to the top rope. He passed above my head until hanging about thirty feet clear of the rock, prevented from swinging further out by the fact that the bottom of the rope was tied to a piton secured in the Flake above my head. Then he started to move up, the rope jerking wildly each time he thrust up on his etrier; it was a slow and tiring business to climb that pitch. Presently he was silhouetted against the sky, a good eighty feet above me. Ten minutes later, he shouted down. I was to release the first haul bag. I lowered it out on a trail of rope until it hung thirty feet clear of the rock, then shouted for Don to pull it up, hoping that it wouldn't entangle with the jumar rope where they both disappeared over the lip of the overhang. It went well, however, and the second one followed likewise. I then started up myself, experiencing the strange sensation of climbing away from the rock as I moved my jumars upwards, like a boat on its painter drifting out from the jetty. Presently I hung vertically beneath the 'roof', sliding one jumar up after the other whilst the safety lamp slid behind on another corlene safety rope, which was now the worse for wear. I let the cine camera dangle down below my feet and obtained some sensational film of a green world far below, spinning in slow motion. It seemed that the lip of the overhang grew no closer, but the gap between myself and the red rock did diminish gradually : ten feet ... eight feet ... six feet ... I paused and looked up again. I was appalled to see that the rope was badly frayed. The innards of the sheathed rope were visible, like entrails, for the casing was completely cut through. When I next moved the clamp up, the sheath slipped down with it, as if I was skinning a rabbit. I remained still and tried to control my panic. Would it hold? I asked myself. As far as I could see, most of the core was intact but it measured only about a quarter of an inch in diameter, under the strain. I shouted urgently up to Don.

'Hey, Don! – the bloody rope's almost cut through.'

'What's that, Jock?'

'The rope,' I shouted. 'It's badly frayed; the sheath's gone.'

'Aye, so I see,' his head appeared instantly, his blue cap pulled down over his eyes like a guardsman. There was more than the usual amount of academic interest in his voice: 'You'd better get a move on before it parts.'

Another strand went. I gasped, looking up anxiously. I had shifted the top jumar on to the bare core of the rope and the sheath was bunched up in the grip of the lower one, like the rubber bellows on a hydraulic ram.

'I'm going to try and clip the lower jumar on to the other corlene rope,' I continued.

Don was only about ten feet above me, poised on a tiny ledge with the haul bags hanging below him, like Santa Claus negotiating a suitable chimney.

'That's a bit tatty as well,' he warned.

'I'll have to use it – I can't get the upper jumar over the lip of the overhang; the top side of the frayed sheath is preventing it.'

Finally I managed to remove the bottom jumar and clip it

on to the green corlene rope. This had frayed where it had been pulled over the rough sandstone edge. Alternating between the two ropes, I shifted the top jumar up on to the sound section of rope above the damage, and breathed a sigh of relief. I looked down between my feet and saw where I would probably have landed, 900 feet below amidst the bromeliad avalanche at the bottom of the face. I slid the jumars up until I had gained a ledge about three inches wide on which I placed my right boot and hung back on my harness, limp with relief.

'You know, Don, I've come to the conclusion that this is a dangerous climb!' I observed unnecessarily.

'Well, the reason I took so long climbing up this pitch was that I hammered the sharp edge away with my Whammer to try and make it smoother. The rock's like sandpaper.'

I was glad that I had taken the precaution of bringing a new 11 mm. rope of Mo's with me. 'Can I join you on your ledge?' I asked Don.

'No room here, mate – it's only six inches wide.'

I didn't fancy hanging where I was for long, it wasn't exactly comfortable. We wondered how Mo and Joe were doing. We couldn't see them, but could hear lots of shouting. They were in the Bottomless Chimney and sounded as if they were gripped up.

They certainly were. Mo had gone into the lead again when he reached his high point and put a bolt in to step into the chimney. He continues the drama:

There was a real awkward bit; then the next twenty foot was a piece of piss and I thought: 'Oh, great, we've cracked it ...' I brought Joe up and it was getting a bit damp. When I started on the next pitch it was just piss; in minutes, I was soaked to the skin. The vegetation was nasty, prickly stuff, with blind, shallow cracks. Time was being eaten away; I eventually reached a stance and found that it had taken three and a half hours to lead the last section. I was feeling tired and it was a bloody awful stance into the bargain. I hammered a bolt in a short way, and a couple of nuts for good measure. I wasn't too happy about the stance, but I heaved the ropes into position and called on Joe to come up.

So Joe started up, and was appalled at the state of the route. He commented:

It was like the Black Cleft on Cloggy, except that it overhung more, and there was certainly more vegetation. I was getting cold, as well as soaked, and had started to shiver violently. When I reached Mo, he too, was shivering uncontrollably and asked me to lead through. I had half expected this and didn't relish the thought. At the time, Mo was hanging out from his stance – there wasn't room to lean against the rock – and had one foot in an etrier. It looked to me as if there might be a ledge about forty feet up on the right, just above where the Bottomless Chimney narrows.

'If there's a ledge up there, we could use it for a bivvy,' I said to him, and set off. The cracks were terrible. All the pegs I put in were loose. Things were as bad as they could possibly be: the cracks were either very thin ones, really shallow, so that the knife blades went in only a short way, or they were bong cracks which were V-shaped and great care had to be used in putting weight on them. Water was pouring over me all the time and I soon saw that the ledge which I had spotted from below was nothing more than a tiny step in the rock, about eight inches wide. A huge insect scuttled effortlessly and insultingly across the wall.

Mo had watched Joe on this section with concern:

He got gripped up there – I got gripped watching him, wondering about that belay of mine. He got piss wet in that bloody channel. By this time I was feeling really bad and I just couldn't stop shivering. Joe had been three hours on the pitch. I kept getting cramp and snapping my legs out; eventually he shouted down that he was feeling bad. We realized it was five o'clock and too late to try again. I lowered Joe off his top peg – a doubtful one – and he joined me. We shouted down and told Hamish and Don that we were baling out.

I had thought it tough, hanging from my jumars for six and a half hours, but my hardships were minimal compared to those suffered by Mo and Joe. I regarded the luxuriant vegetation which hung down like huge clusters of grapes beside me like the Gardens of Babylon. Parakeets nesting in the hanging gardens were seeking refuge for the approaching night. Since about three o'clock the weather had been getting steadily worse. It was now blowing a full gale and both Don and I were being buffeted by the south-easterly wind. Rain accompanied the wind; horizontal rain droplets gleaming in the light like tracer bullets. The heavy rope, hanging from my harness, flew out at right-angles to the face, tugging at me violently. It was the worst weather we had encountered yet.

I had asked Don the time about half an hour before as I sensed it was growing late, so we were both mentally prepared for retreat when Mo's voice reached us over the wind.

'That's it, then,' said Don gruffly. 'It's down.'

I passed one end of the rope which was tied to my harness up to Don, and unclipped my figure-of-eight for the descent. I put a karabiner on to the corlene rope, also, and clipped it to a sling from my harness so that it would guide me into Africa Flake, otherwise I should be left hanging out in space. I lowered myself down, the weight of my body forcing the rope from the wind's grasp as I descended.

At Africa Flake, I tied it off at the bottom end and shouted back to Don to lower the first haul bag. My shout was snatched greedily by the wind and I got no response. But Don had seen the weight and tension ease off the new rope and knew that I was safely lodged on the Flake. Soon the haul bag appeared, coming towards me through the gloom, like the descending foot of an elephant.

I was now partially sheltered from the rain under the great roof, but up on that wet stance the other two were in dire straits. When Joe reached Mo's stance, he later described it as 'one of the worst grips of my life'. There was a tangled morass of rope and gear. Thirteen ropes hung down from this point and, in the confusion, it was impossible to tell which was which. Belayed by Mo, Joe just climbed down this bundle of ropes until he could determine which were the two fixed ones. About forty or fifty feet down, he reached a point where he could just see what he was doing in the failing light, and flicked a nut into a crack to belay himself whilst he sorted things out.

Above him, Mo knew that if he had to abseil down from there, he was going to be in the shit. He was so knackered that he shouted down to Joe to tell Don to wait on the stance, in case he needed some assistance.

Joe continued down and came round the corner at the bottom of the chimney in what he called 'a really gripping position'. Don was just preparing to go when Joe stopped him to wait for Mo.

It was the most frightening place any of us had ever been on rock, or rather, hanging off rock : a little more actual contact would have been reassuring! It would be difficult to imagine a more hair-raising situation. The weather was growing wilder, the wind plucked savagely at us and a full scale drama was in progress. It was now a fight for survival – each of us was accompanied by the numbed thought that one little mistake could lead to disaster and possible tragedy.

'I'll carry on down, Don,' said Joe. 'I don't feel so good.'

'Okay.'

Joe automatically attached his figure-of-eight in preparation for that nasty abseil down from the roof on to the two ropes which he had climbed up. As he launched himself over the edge he felt the frayed rope under his hand as he fed it through the descendeur. He didn't know then that I had had such a narrow escape on the ascent and that the rope had almost parted. In the darkness, Don hadn't realized which ropes he was using. Joe had been about to descend on two ropes; a loose corlene used for sack hauling, which was hanging over a bromeliad beside Don – not anchored – and the faulty rope which had already scared the daylights out of me! Quick as a flash, he saw his mistake and attached a jumar above the damaged section of rope, then moved up and transferred to the new rope. It was a very close thing.

Mo was now coming down towards Don and was exhausted by the time he reached the bottom of the loop, and he had to move 'uphill' to gain Don's stance. Don gave him a fag and he felt better after a short rest. He then continued down the big abseil and joined Joe at Africa Flake. Joe was having a hard time, trying to transfer the first haul bag so that he could lower it down to me on the Terrace. In the end he simply cut through three slings and transferred it to the lower rope which led from the Flake down to Tarantula Terrace.

Don began to lower the top haul bag but, in the confusion and high wind, it was impossible to tell him which rope to use. As a result, he lowered it on a rope which only allowed it to descend forty feet; it was marooned away from the face: ninety pounds' weight swinging like a ponderous pendulum. The answer to this predicament could only have been found by Don – he began abseiling and, approaching the lip of the roof, caught hold of and tied the haul bag to his harness. He then proceeded to abseil down, with his weighty trophy dangling below him. It was clipped on to the abseil rope and eventually reached Africa Flake ahead of Don, where it was fielded by Mo. As Mo said later: 'Don was probably more gripped than I'd ever seen him before.'

Back at Camp 7 they could hear our shouts above the howling of the wind, and wondered what was amiss. There was obviously some kind of crisis!

We were well and truly soaked, mentally beaten, and utterly exhausted. As for Mo and Joe, their hands were torn in shreds, while nails, eyelashes, and hair were caked with mud. There was mud even inside our helmets and our eyes were constantly sore, aggravated by debris and lichen from the cracks. Even our sleeping bags were wet, inside the haul bags. The waterfalls began to roar, competing with the wind, as we huddled over a small Gaz stove and prepared some soup. Don didn't bother with more, but retired to his hideout on the other side of the Prow. The rest of us ate a tin of meat. I contacted Camp 7 on the walkie-talkie and gave Neil a brief rundown on our defeat, promising to call him in the morning, when we had things sorted out a bit.

'Okay, blue,' he replied. 'Best of luck.'

The violence of that storm was almost unbelievable. It was as if we were cradled in the rigging of a sailing ship, with the wind tearing at the shrouds.

Meanwhile, things had been quieter and happier down at Camp 7. Adrian had come up and established a new camp above Camp 7; this was known as Camp 7½. It lay between Alex's filming shelter and El Dorado swamp, a much pleasanter spot than Camp 7. There was a shelter for Ragu, too. Despite his earlier protestations of being unable to go above Camp 6, he had been lured on by tales of the fabulous flora. Like a true scientist, he put personal discomfort aside in deference to duty. Adrian took up to Camp 7½ the still sealed bag of First Day Covers for the Guyana GPO, ready to go into action the moment we set foot on the summit. Chocolate had been brought in by Indian porters and Alex found a secret cache of it – hidden by Jonathan – which he and Gordon joyfully raided. Alex also had, at long last, his change of clothing: in the sixth week of the expedition!

As so often, after a storm, the morning dawned fine and clear. I almost felt I could reach out and touch Kukenaam. Don was still lying in his bag – a remote and horizontal orange rectangle resembling a doormat. I got up and packed my hammock in a haul bag; then took the rest of my posssessions round to where Joe and Mo were still sleeping. Next I collected some water. There was no problem this morning:

every bromeliad was full, but I didn't even have to molest them, because the cut-off plastic containers were overflowing and I filled two dixies for our morning brew.

By this time, Joe's head had appeared round the flysheet.

'Morning,' he croaked, commencing the throat-clearing ritual which took about five minutes and was very unproductive. Mo groaned in his hammock and started to complain about Brown's movements which disturbed his sleep. Don came round – an excellent sense of timing – just as the billy was boiling.

'I suppose we're going down?' I boldly asked the vital question which was hanging in the air.

'I am,' said Joe.

'Yes, we should have a council of war down below,' Mo suggested.

We didn't speak much over breakfast; we were a bit vague and still numbed from the previous night's experiences. We drank the tea, took a mouthful of porridge, and then sorted out gear for the descent. I noticed that Joe packed all his possessions, leaving nothing behind on the ledge. He started off down and we all followed after. I carried back my sleeping bag, hammock, and the exposed cine film, leaving the rest of my equipment, and the cine cameras, hanging from pegs under the overhang.

Lieutenant Mike and Maurice 'the Spy' were in residence at Camp 8. They had a fine selection of food: we were offered cheese and biscuits, and coffee with sugar and milk. Things were really looking up now!

I changed into my cane cutter's boots and then Mo and I set off down with Joe. Don lingered on the ledge for a while, taking advantage of the sun to dry his equipment. He had eventually met up with his climbing harness, only to discover that it was now far too large for him!

'You know, Don,' I pointed out as he tried it for size. 'We could make a fortune; running expeditions for obese tourists.

Just take them up to 20,000 feet, give them no food, and they'd lose a couple of stones in a week.'

The trail between Camp 8 and 7½ must be one of the worst in the world, but after the sheer vertical height of the face, it seemed wonderful. Simply to be able to move again without sliding jumars up a rope, or using a descendeur, was incredibly relaxing. I was feeling much better already.

Neil had the camera all set up for interviews on our arrival at Camp 7½. We found Adrian, looking tired but well. There were a number of Indians too; Maurice was back with the main party and looking, I thought, rather sad at the loss of Mike, after the accident. Jonathan was also at Camp 7½ and generously volunteered to return to Camp 6, with Mike Atherley and Maurice Barrow, to leave enough room for the four of us. There was plenty of food and another air drop was expected soon. Plastic dustbins, filled with pitcher plants, were being tended with loving care by Ragu, wearing a shirt which would have rivalled Mike's for rents and stains; his trousers were in a similar disgraceful state.

An hour or so later Don rolled into camp, looking fresh and tidy. He had had a wash in the pool at the base of the face.

'How-do,' he greeted his co-leader.

Don and I then moved down to Camp 7 to share the camp with Neil and his two companions, where Cham was also ensconced. Mo and Joe decided to remain at Camp 7½ with Adrian; there was just enough room for them, though Mo would have to sleep on the deck. I went ahead, squelching through calf-deep mud towards El Dorado Swamp. I was feeling fine now, fortified by a good meal, and sang merrily :

'Mud, mud, glorious mud, nothing quite like it for cooling the blood.'

Cham was already at the radio, sending out news of our defeat to his Government. The Roraima story was gaining world interest. Though we didn't realize it, Cham had latent journalistic genius. Alex caught an inkling of it when he heard Cham sending out a message the evening of the air drop. It ran something like this: 'Zero Delta, Zero Delta. Airdrop successful. I say again airdrop successful. In the words of an ex-RAF authority, the airdrop was a superb piece of flying, I say again...'

What Alex had actually said was:

'In the opinion of an ex-RAF ablution orderly, that's the best bit of flying I've seen,' as he watched the daring manoeuvres of Chan-A-Sue. In fact, Cham could be relied upon to provide comic relief at regular intervals ... Alex usually sent out his exposed film stock – the rushes – with my *Observer* report, but there was always a delay in returning them from London to Georgetown, where the Government authorities would vet them. They were actually reaching London at the same time as my articles. He couldn't understand this delay, and in exasperation christened the returned film the 'slowies'; the rushes going out and the slowies coming back. Cham overheard these light-hearted remarks and, the very next morning, in his radio message to his HQ, he was blithely requesting information on the 'slowies'.

The newspaper reports of our defeat, which we obtained later, were most amusing:

Roraima Climbers Fail Again:

The mountain has once again defied the skills and bravery of the joint British/Guyana expedition. The team, comprising some of the world's foremost climbers, were driven back by suspected poisonous scorpions and tarantulas ...

Roraima climbers defeated by the last 3,000 feet

... The climbers were expected to reach the top by last weekend, but encountered heavy rains and a temperature below 60° Fahrenheit which took a heavy toll on them. Attempting the last 3,000 feet, the renowned mountaineers could no longer find crevices into which they could drive in *pylons* [sic]. Numerous scorpions and deadly tarantulas which live in the vegetation on the sheer rock face attacked the climbers. Meantime, another member of the expedition, Mike Thompson, who had his feet sliced by sharp grass growing on the face of the mountain and was flown back to the city, is expected to leave for London to-day . . .

That night we all slept well, feeling agreeably full for the first time in weeks.

Though it was pleasantly relaxing in the camps below the face, we all knew that a decision would have to be made sooner or later. Joe was quite adamant that he wasn't going to lead again, but I thought there was a chance he might see things differently in a couple of days. As Mo later said, 'I knew it was very tricky with Joe. I didn't want to start pushing him into a definite decision at this stage. He had made it quite plain that he didn't want to go in front, but I had a hunch that he'd change his mind on the bloody face . . .'

We discussed the political aspects of the expedition. It was obvious now that our impressions – that there were political undertones – were correct. Only the other day, Maurice Barrow had sent off a message to the Government without asking Adrian.

'I suppose that if we get up we will have established access to the Guyana section of the summit,' I said to no one in particular. 'We're just pawns in a political game of chess. All that palava with the Government departments in Georgetown.'

'Don't I know it,' said Neil. 'But I suppose we have a reasonable deal – without the support of the GDF, we wouldn't have got far, would we?' They had certainly been efficient. Later, I remarked jokingly to Adrian, 'You should give me honorary Guyanese citizenship for going to the top, Adrian. Wouldn't that substantiate the Guyanese right of access?'

'I am very well aware of that, Hamish,' Adrian responded seriously.

Alex was kept hard at it by Neil. Cham had caught a snake

and an aggressive spider, so Alex continued his 'X Certificate' work. We heard also that a large snail had been captured by Mike Tamessar at Camp 6. Mike had been unable to remain at Camp 7 since a heart complaint, which he had suffered from in the past, began to play up again. The snail was about ten inches long and Neil was determined to film it. Alex, however, was still very weak and felt unable to make the journey back down through the slime forest. Obviously, he was being pressed too hard, so Adrian came up with the common-sense solution that the snail should be brought up to Camp 7 to be immortalized. Neil himself was much fitter now; he had lost a great deal of weight and was moving between camps at the least excuse. He had been up and down to Camp 6 six times already!

Meanwhile Cham had developed what looked like Achilles tendon trouble, so I found a crêpe bandage for him.

The next morning Mo came down to our camp. It was time to talk ... There was a continuous undercurrent of hostility between Mo and Don now. Mo sat down on a twisted Bonnetia branch inside the shelter and sipped his tea from a yellow plastic mug.

'I've been talking with Joe ...'

'Aye,' Don said non-committally.

'We feel that you should lead to the summit now.'

'Oh? You mean that, as soon as things get a bit tough, you want to back out?' started Don aggressively.

'I don't mind taking another turn leading,' I volunteered. 'I've got my boots and harness now, and it doesn't look as if we'll get much film on the next bit – too wet.'

'I don't mean that at all,' Mo hotly refuted Don's accusations. 'Joe and I are both completely buggered and it'll be some days before we're fit enough to go back, anyhow – that is, if I can persuade Joe. Why don't you come up and have a natter with him? It'll probably help.'

'Aye, we'll take a turn up later,' said Don, folding up a letter which he had been reading when Mo arrived.

I took my sleeping bag and hammock with me and accompanied Don up to 7½ an hour or so later. The camp appeared to have been built inside a barbed wire entanglement – so thick was the Bonnetia – but it was quite comfortable. Mo had been sleeping on a mattress of heather-like material. Adrian had slung his hammock up in the centre of a shelter, and Joe's hung limply, precariously attached to a thin, twisted sapling. With Joe's weight inside, it must have resembled a fully-tensioned catapult.

I was greeted by Joe and Adrian with an offer of soup – even a choice of soup – dispensed by Adrian's efficient and pleasant 'butler', Arnold, who addressed us all as Uncle, except Adrian, who was Mr Thompson.

We discussed things at length with Joe. He seemed to be feeling better already and agreed to go up with Mo, providing Don and I got up the next section. Mo was reluctant to do any more leading just now, and understandably was feeling hurt by Don's remarks. Nothing was going to be achieved unless some progress was made on the route during the next few days. Food supplies were again running low. There was such a large party to feed that our predicament resembled Britain's balance of payments – always at crisis level.

Don dislikes being forced into sudden action. At about midday I set off for the face with a couple of Indians. There was plenty I could do on my own until he came up. The day was fine and it seemed as if the weather was taking a turn for the better. When the sun came out, it was extremely hot. I was suddenly aware that the Equator wasn't far away, despite the cold conditions we experienced on the face and at night-time.

At Camp 8 I started to dismantle the bivouac; we would have no further use for it. The vertical trail was now well established to Tarantula Terrace and it would represent our new base camp. I had finished working when Don arrived. We had a brew and then he led up the fixed ropes. We carried enough food with us for about five days, as well as some extra rope. This was the last of the rope. With the exception of a small amount used in making shelters, 4,000 feet of corlene alone would have been used by the end of expedition.

I followed Don up the Big Diedre but the rope felt slack as I clipped on to it for the last pitch below the Terrace. When I reached the top of the chimney, where one had to move right on a small shelf, I discovered that the anchor peg had come out. The rope was now hanging from a higher peg in the wall leading up to Africa Flake. Fortunately, we had taken the necessary precaution of tying all the ropes together so that they were continuous from our highest point down to Camp 8.

It was a fine evening and we ate a meat curry for dinner.

'Quite pleasant to be back, Don,' I remarked. 'I think I'll doss in my usual place . . . Are you staying here?'

We had been cooking at the overhang previously occupied by Mo and Joe.

He decided he might as well and could use Mo's hammock. Before retiring with my rucksack for an early night, I shouted back as I went round on the fixed rope to my haven, 'Hey, Don, anything to say to the others? – I'll call them at nine o'clock on the walkie-talkie.'

'Aye, give them my love . . .'

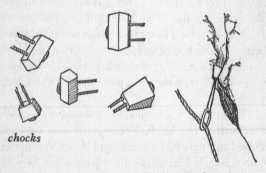

chocks

chock in crack

Chapter 11

'Will you have a cigarette, mate?' said the Leader
of the Push,
'I'll have the bloody packet!' said the bastard of
the bush.

'The Bastard of the Bush', *Henry Lawson*

It was a delightful morning. A humming bird hovered in front of my hammock as if chiding: 'Get up, you lazy slob.' The parakeet squadron chattered excitedly all around whilst in the remote distance, I could hear the voices of the Indians at Camp 7½. With a sense of anticipation I got up and joined Don. Porridge and tea fortified us for the day's activities.

The commuter's route up the overhangs seemed to deteriorate, rather than improve, with usage. More ropes were showing signs of fraying but I had expected this and had taken the precaution of carrying a couple of empty kit bags in my rucksack: I hoped to cover the sharp edges and so prevent excessive rope abrasion. I occupied the stance where Don had held his long and cold vigil the day of the big rout, whilst he continued on up the Bottomless Chimney. On the way up I had fixed the kit bags under two vulnerable ropes, securing them with lengths of cord attached to pitons. The ropes were now protected at Africa Flake. But at the top of the Great Roof, I led only the new rope over the bag since the other rope looked as if it had had it.

Above me a continuous stream of shouts and curses floated down: 'what a cock up' a familiar phrase – 'Half hitches, blooming – half hitches . . .!' Don had been infuriated by my habit of tying the end of the fixed ropes off in half hitches many a time; Joe, also, was guilty of this crime. Don liked to be able to see what was going on and it annoyed him to reach a stance, only to be confronted with a mass of knots. On the other hand, I am almost fastidiously tidy by nature and I couldn't resist tidying up the loose ends. However, I knew I wasn't responsible for this latest misdemeanour.

'Can I come up?' I shouted hopefully.

No reply. I tried again five minutes later: still no reply.

'I'm coming down,' his voice echoed dully as if it had come from the depths of a wet cave. He appeared on the steep edge above me: a bedraggled figure dripping with water. I pulled him in; he was hanging at the bottom of the fixed rope, above the big overhang.

When he had recovered his breath, I asked him:

'What's up?'

'I'll belay you from here; that stance is useless. But the climbing rope's stuck. There are ropes everywhere up there – I've never seen anything like it! I've coiled them up now, but Joe's rope jammed when I tried to pull it down.'

Joe had been lowered from his high point by Mo and had untied from this rope when he had joined Mo at the stance. This would enable the next person climbing to use it as a protection to gain his high point again, using it as a pulley. Don had considered this hideous pitch and decided that it would be better to break off left from the stance, to gain the line he had previously advocated which was much drier. Now Joe's rope had caught: the end of it had snagged close to the top peg as Don pulled impatiently on it. He carried the other end with him; there was only about twenty feet of slack and it was about 130 feet to Joe's high point from where we stood.

'What the hell am I supposed to do now?' I demanded.

'Go up to the stance, and climb out left from there.'

'What am I going to use for rope?'

'Well, you could try and get Joe's rope down; you might manage,' he suggested lamely. 'Or use one of the others up there.'

I pointed out that Mo had said it was best for Don to belay me from up there.

'I don't think so,' he replied, clipping on to the anchor with a karabiner 'It's bloody awful and wet.'

'Anyhow,' I said resignedly. 'I'll go and take a look.'

To leave our present stance necessitated clipping on to the two ropes leading upwards, with a karabiner and sling attached to my harness. Initially the jumars operated almost horizontally on the other rope, until I could gain the point where the rope started to hang vertically from above. Care has to be exercised in operating the jumar clamps in this manner, since they are designed for ascending vertical, or near vertical, ropes – not horizontal ones. In fact, in this case, I was quite secure as I had a karabiner and safety sling running on the other rope. At first I moved about twelve feet away from a rib of rock which bounded the left hand side of the Bottomless Chimney. Soon the rope led me into the chimney and it started to drip ... gently at first: pitter-patter, pitter-patter. But, by the time I was halfway up, it was like climbing up a waterfall. It was wet, vegetated, and thoroughly nasty; and I didn't envy the task which had fallen to Mo and Joe: too much like the mucking out of Augeas' stables. The ledge at the top of the fixed rope was about the size of a paperback novel; it was separated from the main channel, where Joe's rope was hanging, by a small edge of rock. There was a good deal of truth in Don's complaint: there were ropes everywhere, although now, thanks to him, there was some semblance of order. I clipped directly on to the expansion bolt which Mo had placed and leant back, tugging at Joe's rope which led up into the narrows of the water channel. It was definitely jammed but, I thought sourly, no doubt if I risked putting weight on it, it would come down soon enough!

I had a look to the left at the line which Don had suggested, and made a few tentative moves there, but I found that the cracks were blind below the undergrowth. Everything was slimy and horrid. Without bolting, it wouldn't be possible to move left, I was sure. So I looked upwards again, examining more closely the pegs which Joe had used to reach his high point. They didn't look particularly brilliant. Next I studied the pile of ropes. Most of them had been gathering dust in Joe's garret for the past fifteen years and, though possibly adequate to use as fixed rope in conjunction with the corlene, they certainly were not suitable for climbing. It was doubtful if any could have taken severe dynamic loading, and nearly everyone of them had a flaw. As fixing rope, this was unimportant since the dubious parts could be knotted so that they were bypassed, or even cut out altogether. Reluctantly, I came to the conclusion that the only rope suitable was that which hung above me, like the sword of Damocles. Then I had a brainwave. If I were to attach the jumar clamp, upside down, on to the rope and then climb up (the rope was still threaded through dubious pegs), I would be held by the jumar if Joe's jammed rope suddenly pulled free. For a jumar can only move on the rope in one direction; by putting it upside down on Joe's rope, there would be more chance of it holding me if I fell off, since it would then be facing the correct position for loading it. I knew full well that the breaking strain of such devices was a mere 1,600 lb., and that even a short fall could easily generate that loading.

I shouted my intentions down to Don and asked him to tie-off the bottom end of Joe's rope. Then I began to move up the dripping rock, using the pegs as handholds and clipping an etrier to them each time I swapped the jumars from one gap to the next, between pegs. Conditions were so unpleasant that I was scarcely aware of being more scared than normal for a difficult pitch. Water poured in via my anorak hood, and out again at the bottom of my waterproof trousers; it didn't take long to fill my boots. I reached the narrows where Joe had put in an aluminium bong: most of it was sticking out of the crack and it had been bullied up into a corner, to remain there as much by faith as by design. By this time I had almost reached his high point. Suddenly there was a 'ping' and I swung backwards on the bong. The elusive loose end of the rope dangling tantalizingly in front of my eyes, like an eel pulled out of the water. I quickly grasped it, tied on to it, and then yelled to Don. 'Belay me on the climbing rope now, Don. I've got the end!'

Wonders will never cease, was my immediate reaction when I heard him call back 'Okay' in response to my shout.

I breathed a sigh of relief and relaxed on my etrier. I was reasonably safe now and suddenly felt empty as the strain of the past hour hit me. It was not the ideal place to experiment with new ideas. I moved up on Joe's last peg and immediately understood why he was reluctant to continue. The full force of the cataract was concentrated in the next few feet; the chimney formed a corner, the left hand wall jutting out for several feet to form a pillar. Round this corner I discovered the other groove line which we had previously contemplated using. Glancing to my right, I saw the beginning of a small ledge. I didn't know then that Joe had reached this particular ledge and found it useless, so I traversed across, the rope dragging very badly. I found little more than a large foothold and the exposure was alarming. I seemed to be poised on the brink of a rock, while everything beneath was undercut: it was a sobering experience. I moved thankfully back to the 'grand canal'.

I had no rope left so I decided to belay from a bridged position in the narrows of the chimney and bring Don up. Swiftly I put in another peg.

'Come up now, Don,' I yelled at the top of my voice. Far below I could see some activity in the BBC shelter above Camp 7½. They were obviously getting some film today with their telephoto lenses. I shouted again, impatiently:

'Don, the rope's all played out – you'll have to come back up to the high stance.'

There was some grumbling from below but, after a time, I felt the rope slackening a bit and gathered that he was ascending. He came into sight at the base of the Bottomless Chimney. Looking down the Bottomless Chimney was one of the most frightening experiences I have ever had on a mountain (an estimation shared by Joe and the others). One seemed to be dangling helplessly above the jungle. Don moved up gradually, as if a baited fish hook was being reeled in, out of the measureless sea formed by the rain forest. He looked up at me:

'Sorry about that. It looks as if I would have been better staying up at the high stance.'

'If you can belay there now, I'll move up a bit – but I feel pretty grim after that last pitch.'

'Aye, okay; give me ten minutes to get organized.'

With plenty of rope now, and much less drag, I moved on up. The pegging was easy, once I got down to the rock surface, and there were fewer scorpions in the vegetation, though I killed several spiders. I attempted to move left, out of the water-course, and found, to my joy, a superb horizontal crack which led on to the edge of the vertical pillar. As I worked my way round – relatively safely now, on good pegs – I looked with some interest at my surroundings. To my right was a large overhang, just on the other side of the chimney, where I spied a centipede about 7 inches long which gave the place a homely feeling. We were all accustomed to the 'beasties' now; possibly over-confident, as none of us had been bitten yet.

I estimated it was about twenty feet to the tiny ledge below the Green Tower and it should be perfectly dry if we could keep to the pillar. But it was after four o'clock and we didn't want a repetition of the last time. Before preparing to descend, however, I wanted just to have a look at the other groove on the left of the far side of the pillar. I put a few pegs in and moved round, standing on an etrier. Though it looked drier, it was difficult to decide whether to climb into it, when we returned, or to continue up the pillar. Anyhow, I decided that the immediate aim should be to get back down to Tarantula Terrace before dark.

Accordingly, I abseiled off a sound peg, anchored by a

sling and karabiner at my high point, on a single rope, but remained clipped to the climbing rope which was threaded up through the other 'crabs'. This meant I would be guided in by each of Joe's pegs and could easily remove them as I went. Once more I was soaked to the skin, and found it very hard work after the gruelling day. By the time I reached Don there were only four pegs left in position; on my return I could either jumar back up this rope, or on the rope which I had used for the abseil and which hung directly down from my highest point. I tied the abseil rope off at Don's belay.

'I'll carry on down, seeing I'm ready,' I said.

'Aye, okay,' he answered, trying to coax some smoke out of a saturated cigarette.

With my heart in my mouth, I completed the three long abseils down to Tarantula Terrace. From the Great Roof, the abseil was on a single rope running over my strategically placed kit bag. It was the new 11 mm., but unfortunately I had omitted to tell Don that the green corlene rope hanging alongside couldn't be used for abseiling as it went under the kit bag. When he reached this stage (I was by that time safely on the Terrace, preparing a brew), he threaded the corlene safety rope, as well as the new one, through his figure-of-eight. The inevitable result was that, when he lowered himself over the awesome brink, he found a kit bag trying to get through his descendeur. Down below, I could hear every well chosen word with devastating clarity:

'Of all the stupid cock-ups I've ever seen, this takes the candle ...' This monologue continued at least fifteen minutes: the duration of his predicament. Don is always well equipped with gadgetry; a spring-loaded chain for his enormous bunch of keys and, a more recent acquisition, a stapler for the instant repair of wounds. His Swiss knife (which, I must admit, I have found useful in many far-flung corners of the world) now came into play and he severed the offending kit bag from its anchorage with decisive slashes, never once letting up a stream of derisive invective directed at me. I watched it floating out over the rain forest, like a newspaper dropped from the porthole of an ocean liner.

He joined me a short time later.

'You buggered off at a great speed of knots, didn't you?' he said accusingly.

'Had to get a brew on,' I excused myself.

'How the hell did you get down over the Big Roof? I've come to the conclusion that it was impossible. One rope went over the kit bag while the other went under it!'

'I used just the one rope: the new one. The green one was too tatty and it doesn't have enough slack to abseil on now.'

(It had been shortened several times since it was first fixed, due to abrasion from the lip of the Great Roof.)

'Well, I don't know ...' Don spat out, unclipping his jumars. 'People have got some fancy ideas on this trip!'

We had a good night at Tarantula Terrace. We were very tired and sleep came instantly. The morning dawned clear, but it looked as if it would turn wet later. At 5.45 a.m. we heard the distant drone of the Islander's engines. Then, at 6.30 a.m., it was suddenly close at hand. Chan-A-Sue must have been watching the ridge from the distance for, the instant it cleared, he appeared below us; from above it looked as if he must surely crash. He was flying straight towards the Prow and we only caught sight of him for a fleeting moment in that brief clearing of the cloud. But he must have been able to see the faint outline of the Prow for he flew so close that he almost touched the top of Cham's aerial at El Dorado Swamp. A host of packages were disgorged – gifts from heaven – then he flipped the plane over on its right and it side-slipped down into the Waruma watershed, missing the ridge, which rose up steeply above camp, by a hair-breadth fraction. I recalled the words of St Matthew: 'Whence should we have so much bread in the wilderness, as to fill so great a multitude?'

'I've seen some good bush flying in New Zealand,' I said to Don. 'But that takes the cake!'

'Aye, it's nice to watch a chap who's good at his job . . . no bugging about, no flap.'

Chan made several more spectacular runs, then, with an exuberant roar from the depths of the dense cloud turned tail for Georgetown. As a final gesture he dropped a red flare, a friendly glowing light as it fell through the cloud. I think that, in a large measure, we owe the final success of the expedition to Chan-A-Sue and his GDF colleagues.

Water was dripping down the face, and we had no dry clothes left, so we decided to have an off day and try to get dried out. Neil contacted me on the radio from Camp 7:

'Do you like Weetabix, blue?'

'Sure,' I said. 'Anything's better than porridge – I could eat it till the cows come home.'

'You may have to, fella! There's a mountain of it just arrived: somebody must have found a bargain lot in Georgetown; we could tile El Dorado Swamp with it. Plenty of chocolate and fags too.'

A minor crisis had occurred for the nicotine addicts. A package containing cigarettes and evaporated milk could not be found. But after an hour's diligent search, it was finally run to earth: a brown coloured package lying in the swamp. Joe surreptitiously shoved an extra carton of cigarettes into his rucksack for use on the face. Later Neil was dismayed to find he was short of cigarettes for he had promised to give some to the Indians. But when he mentioned this to Adrian, Adrian was firm.

'You don't give the Indians cigarettes – you'll spoil them. They just get their own food; nothing else.'

That night, via the walkie-talkie, we told Joe that we planned to move back up to our high point of the day before and try to reach the Green Tower. He and Mo agreed to follow us up, camp the night at Tarantula Terrace, and then push on in the front the following day, bringing with them all the necessary gear for establishing a camp on the Green Tower. It was a few hours' hard labour even to reach the Bottomless Chimney, and one was tired before starting the day's climbing.

That day I had soaked some dried fish which had been carried in by porters. Maurice the Indian had managed to cook it so that was quite edible, but my attempts were disastrous, to put it mildly. Don spat the first mouthful out into space, and in a kindly voice said he didn't feel so hungry after all and fancied an early night.

Next morning the Wall was wetter than ever: water – streaming everywhere. It hadn't rained any more than the usual seven to eight hours, during the night, but, even the overhang above my head was soaking; a thick mist surrounded us. It was late by the time I went round to headquarters.

'Morning, old fruit.'

'Morning,' he replied, lighting his first fag. (I always wondered how he managed to keep his matches dry in a small container, when everything else was saturated.) 'Good morning for the ducks.'

'Never seen it so wet here – what do you think?'

'Looks like a piss-house wall to me.'

We waited to see if it would dry up at all, but it was a forlorn hope. Eventually we decided to go down and have a talk with the others. The four of us could return together. The journey back down the wall now seemed amazingly familiar. Donning our mudbashing boots, we set off down to Camp 7½. They were surprised to see us, but we explained about the rain, which they had, of course, suffered from too.

Joe had regained some of his lost spirits and was ready to return with Mo. The fact that we had emerged on to good rock from the Bottomless Chimney seemed to boost their morale and they were raring to go. By 2 p.m. their packs were ready and we agreed to follow them up as soon as they were established on the Green Tower. They would spend that night on Tarantula Terrace and move up the face next morning, provided things dried out a bit overnight. I decided to remain at 7½ with Adrian, occupying Mo's hollow in the shrubbery, after he had informed me, with the air of a knowledgeable arachnologist, that the spiders were really quite friendly! Don went back to 7, preferring the security of his hammock.

I spent an interesting evening talking with Isaac and Adrian. Isaac had returned to camp that same afternoon, for he had made the journey out to Maiurapai once more, to ensure the regular continuity of supplies. He had also delivered my report for the *Observer*. He made the trip from Camp 7½ to Maiurapai in one day: an incredible achievement. The longer I knew the Indians, the more I respected them. They had fantastic powers of endurance, while their load-carrying ability was as good as any native race I had ever seen.

Neil, seriously affected by his unaccustomed light weight, was dashing to and fro like a two-year-old; always doing jobs and helping generally, much to Don's annoyance. That afternoon he was chopping firewood at Camp 7. The twisted branches were swinish to cut, being both hard and tough. A small axe – the property of the expedition – had been lying in camp for some weeks, in a shockingly blunt state. The Indian, Maurice, sensibly sharpened it when the BBC were out filming next morning. Later in the day, Cham came into the shelter and, between radio schedules, amused himself by plying the file to the axe for a second time. Gordon returned from 7½ ahead of the others. He immediately tackled the task (it had been bothering his orderly mind for a number of days, but he just hadn't had time to do anything about it) for the file was conveniently stuck in a branch beside the axe.

When Alex came into camp, Gordon was sorting out some tapes in his tent; though he heard the rasping of a now bluntened file on the razor sharp edge of the axe, he simply thought it was one of the Indians putting an edge on a cutlass: a task which they performed several times a day. Neil came in last. Feeling the urge for physical activity, he picked up this well-tempered instrument wielding it like Saint Barbatus, and, with the second blow, succeeded in gashing his hand quite badly.

'I didn't know it was so sharp!' he complained, holding up a gory hand for Don's inspection.

'Why can't you mind your own bloody business, Neil,' Don demanded aptly. 'The Indians are much better than you'll ever be at cutting wood – and they're paid for it.'

Don showed no sign of sympathy and didn't even volunteer to use his wound-stapler. Neil accepted Gordon's offer of a clean dressing instead.

At Camp 7½ Adrian related how Joe and Mo had attempted to make cigarettes with the teabags which, like a good Aberdonian, I had hung up after use for a rainy day. Toilet paper and Tetley's tea bags couldn't compete with Virginia tobacco, obviously, and the experiment died in a very lathargic puff. That night Alex saw an opossum under the shelter but it moved off as soon as he got his torch out.

The morning brought better weather and we heard occasional shouts from the face – there was plenty of activity there. Mo and Joe jumared up to our high point, where Mo took the lead:

The first part of the pillar was awkward and I muttered rude things to Joe about Hamish who had left the rope through the pegs: I had to unclip the bloody things. I moved back into the corner crack above. It wasn't too bad there, surprisingly enough; not absolutely pissing down, as it was below. The hard bit was getting on to that ledge below the Green Tower. This took me an hour – it was another bromeliad overhang. The vegetation was horrible and there were those large insects on stilts which looked bloody terrible. I brought Joe up and it looked like a forty feet walk up to the Green Tower, but that took Joe just over an hour.

Until he made that last move, Joe had been ensconced on the nasty stance in the Bottomless Chimney, and not entirely happy:

From that horrible perch, the garbage kept raining down from Mo, as if he was intent on making an instant compost heap. When I was eventually called up, I was very pleasantly surprised to see he was on a good stance with room to move about. But not an ideal place to pitch a camp: the ledge was about six feet by three feet and a steady stream of water poured down from above, en route for the Bottomless Chimney. I looked up; for as far as I could see, there was vertical, dripping rock covered in bloody vegetation. I led through, digging and grovelling, and finally reached the high point of this series of ledges, eventually coming to a fine flat ledge about ten feet long and varying in width from two to four feet. It was protected by rock overhangs.

Mo describes their new bivouac site:

When I joined him, I knew why it had taken Joe so long to climb up that rock garden. The grass and plants gave way under my feet. He had stuck a few pegs in, but had climbed it mainly free. 'Here we are,' I said to Joe. 'On a piss-wet cliff and there's no bloody water for a brew!' Old Brown legs managed to find a drip speck and we put some poly bags there; when we got the wee tent up we felt quite chuffed. I had to sleep on the outside that night as I lost the toss and we got on to the radio and had a natter with Don and Hamish down below. We told them we would let them know tomorrow if there was another ledge higher up, as this one would be a bit cramped for two tents.

Neil and the others came up from Camp 7. They had caught a spider going into Gordon's tent and had spent some time filming it; it proved to be a particularly aggressive one. Alex used a special lens on the Eclair, which could focus down to 2 mm. He swears he saw venom dripping from its fangs.

In the morning Don and I set off to spend the night on Tarantula Terrace. This would be our last trip. Camp 8 looked desolate – a pile of rubbish scattered on the allotment was rapidly being covered over by the vegetation which had been thrown off the face. Before we left Camp 7½, we had seen the two others working their way up, above the Green Tower. It was arranged that they should take a walkie-talkie with them that day, to let us know when they found a ledge which we could use, but their reasons for not contacting us were obvious – later. They were busy!

The day's events were recorded by Mo:

I started off in the morning, straight up above the ledge on the belay pegs. I had only moved one peg up when it flirted out. I think I must have overdriven it and fractured the rock. Next thing I knew, I was down at Brown's level. No harm done: it was only a free fall of a few feet. The next bit wasn't complicated; then I found myself in one of those shitty crackless areas again, and I had to traverse round to the right a bit. Then the vegetation really started. It was the first real vegetation we had to climb; definitely secateurs and wire cutter material. I spent ages on it. The rock went duff into the bargain; forced me to put a bolt in. When I'd finished, that was half an hour gone – a precious half hour!

I was feeling demoralized again. I had thought it was going to be easy, and it wasn't ... Then I made one bolt move, then a peg, and I was in a corner which was easy. Suddenly, I felt elated. I got a really good stance in a cave where I was dry, smashed every spider in sight, and tore the vegetation off as if I was ripping off rotten wallpaper. Joe came up. We felt great now. 'We're bombing it, Baron,' I said exultantly. I had come up 120 feet on that last pitch, which was about the best we had done in that time since we started the climb. Joe led for the next thirty feet up an easy vegetated gully. The rope zipped out. I thought by Christ, we've cracked it now! We couldn't see the top, though, for it was really murky, but we must have been within a couple of hundred feet. I joined Joe and thought, you cunning sod, Brown, for the rock was more difficult above, but he insisted it was the best place to stop. It was easy pegging above and I got on to this brilliant ledge with a roof above: perfect. There was no vegetation so I rammed three really good pegs home and brought him up –

it was only twenty feet – and said: 'Done you, you bugger; it's your turn to lead now!' The next pitch looked hard.

'Do you mind leading?' asked Joe. 'Well, I don't really want to.' 'I know,' he replied. 'But I definitely don't want to.' I didn't want to chance our luck and make an issue of it – I knew he would have led it all right if I'd pushed him into it. He'd already said that he didn't want to lead again on the climb, but had done so without any prompting from me. It was just my luck that it was the most strenuous bloody thing on the whole route. On the first five feet I pulled the pockets off my cagoule and I had a real bloody struggle, grunting, growling, and busting in this squeeze. Then the back of the chimney was mud. I tried putting bongs in. I'd bang them in all right – they'd go right in to the hilt – and I'd just pull on them and out they'd shoot. I did this about five times, getting more and more gripped. Eventually I managed to make a couple of moves and, removing some vegetation, got one in without hitting the back of the shallow crack. The chimney went up for about thirty feet, and then there was a bloody overhang. It stuck out directly above my head – like a mantelpiece – for about five feet. I whammed a bolt in the right hand wall of the groove to see if I could bypass it that way. It was hopeless; bare rock everywhere. I'd have to go up to the roof. The overhang was one of vegetation and I moved up, hoping to get round it, just slightly to the right where it overhung about thirty feet or so. I put a bolt in there and realized that it was getting late, remembering that we were supposed to have contacted the other two on the walkie-talkie. I went down to Joe and we abseiled down to the Green Tower, sorting out the ropes a bit better on the way. It had started to rain about three hours before and we were soaked to the skin and both as black as hell. Back in the tent, that night, we had a bloody lousy time. Everything was soaked, but we consoled ourselves that we would get to the top next day. We called Hamish and Don on the radio . . .

'Hello, Hamish, Mo here,' I got his signal loud and clear. 'Hello, Mo. Had a good day?'
'Oh, the usual grip. Joe and I think we can crack it tomorrow. There's not much room on the Green Tower, but there are good ledges above.'

Somewhere in the background I could hear Joe laughing. 'Don't tell them about the spiders!'

'Did I hear Brown saying something about spiders?' I asked Mo suspiciously.

'No, we've killed them all,' Mo said reassuringly. 'It's a good cave though a bit wet – but there's nothing else.'

'Okay,' I agreed, anxious to conserve the batteries. 'We'll be up tomorrow. See you.'

Don and I got off to a good start. Amongst other things, we took up a plastic container to catch drips. Water was desperately hard to collect on the Green Tower, we had been told. It was, once again, up those nerve-racking ropes. We knew that if this climb was repeated often enough, there would inevitably be an accident. We fervently hoped this would be the last time.

I went on ahead, up the Bottomless Chimney, to see if it would be worthwhile transferring the ropes to the drier groove but, arriving at my earlier high point above the narrows, I quickly realized that it would be too big a job. The Bottomless Chimney was the driest we had seen it, though I got wet anyway, climbing up the ropes; the most direct line of ascent, where the climbing rope hung, was also a channel for the surface water. I struggled with the vegetated overhang which led to the first ledge (Mo's ledge) and turned to pull up the haul bag. This proved a tremendous undertaking. Not only was it very heavy, but the rope cut into the vegetation on the lip of the ledge and it took all my strength to pull it through the undergrowth. The pitch was about 180 feet. Eventually, I resorted to a winching system, using jumars, and successfully landed it: it was like hauling in a heavy anchor single-handed. I shouted for Don to follow. The tent was perched above me on the main ledge of the Green Tower. There was no sign of the others, but plant specimens descending in hordes – often hitting me – indicated the destruction of yet another herbaceous border.

Don went ahead to give me a break.

About ten minutes later, he was at the bivouac ledge and started to pull the sack upwards. I followed behind it, clipped on to the fixed rope. Just before I gained the ledge, up a vertical section of greenery, I noticed the fixed rope hanging in a loop from an overhang above my head. It was tied in at the bottom on belay pegs. To my right, attached to a hardy bromeliad, was one of the most inaccessible water reservoirs I had ever seen: a small sheet of plastic was stretched over the bromeliad which grew on a rock step at the base of the overhang. This step was only about four inches square, and the wall fell away abruptly to the top of the Bottomless Chimney, and space beyond. There wasn't much room for a tent, but we could probably put a flysheet round the overhang. We didn't fancy Mo and Joe's cave of spiders, so decided to make the best of it. I suppose I'd slept in worse places, but not since I was dossing with the beggars in India.

It had been clear for most of the day and we wondered how the others were faring. They had got off early that day, eager to try and reach the summit. Joe takes up the story:

Mo had taken some more bolts with him and, from his high point under the fringe of overhang, he had to use five in order to reach a point where he could start cutting through the vegetation. They were obviously desperate to fix. He was down to the last drill now, if it broke, we would have to pack it in. Once he was in position, he cut a trench through it: great lumps of weird plants went hurtling down into the abyss. It took him two hours to cut a way through. Both of us were completely splattered with mud. I followed him up and found him on a nice terrace. It was about six feet wide and some forty feet long. There was a crack full of some queer growth, leading up to what looked like a ledge above, and Mo volunteered to investigate.

Mo continues the tale:

Joe went over to the right of the stance to have a look, but it was no good. Then he tried the crack a bit closer to me, but came back down and said: 'You have a look, Mo.' I saw that it was possible to traverse back left from the awkward crack he had tried, to a point above the weird vegetation bulge. I think that he was hoping that I'd have a go at it, but I was feeling shagged after the pitch below. He returned to have another go, put a peg in and laybacked with his feet in the etrier and sort of swooped off. His hands still stayed in the same place and he didn't fall off. I suggested he should put a bolt in, so he did, then steamed up thirty feet to a huge ledge. I jumared up and found the next pitch gave me the absolute horrors. It was an overhanging chimney continuing up from a huge block on the ledge. Joe thought he could see light through the hole in the chimney. A through route by the look of things! I went up the chimney, over great loose bricks, and was soon inside a large cave with a window, or rather, a skylight, high in the roof. It wasn't hard; just loose. In fact, it turned out to be some of the easiest climbing on the whole route. We reached another big ledge, plastered with vegetation. The top was just above! 'It can't be more than 200 feet,' I exclaimed to Joe. But it was getting too late to do it that day. The probable route seemed to take the line of a tapering, overhanging chimney, which looked nasty; then up vegetated grooves and walls to reach the top edge. We certainly knew it could be done in a final day of climbing. So we started to descend, tired but elated. Don and Hamish would be on their way up by now.

I was hammering a peg in for the flysheet when a voice with a marked Mancunian accent materialized from outer space:

'How do?'

It was Joe, hanging free from the rock in the middle of a loop of rope.

'Hiya, Jo. Did you make it?' asked Don, peering up from beneath his cap skip.

'One pitch to go. We were only about 200 feet from the top!'

He had no sooner swung in than we saw the rope jerk upwards as Mo clipped on above. Joe looked all in. His face was pallid and drawn, a strained look in his eyes. He was, besides, soaked, shivering, and covered in mud. I don't think I have ever seen anyone quite so completely covered in muck in all my days of climbing. He looked as if he had just come back from a week's potholing stint. I helped him stow his wet gear in a spongy mass at the back of the ledge. Mo swung round the overhang and dangled out in front of us at the landing stage.

'Good to see you blokes. Nice bit for you to lead tomorrow, Hamish.'

'Great,' I said. 'Looking forward to that: I hope I can get up.'

I think that Mo and Joe had mixed feelings about us sharing the few square feet still available in front of their tent, that night. Though they welcomed our company, there wasn't enough water and there certainly wasn't room to move.

'We'll have to turn by numbers tonight, Don,' I commented, observing the eighteen inch wide space which remained for us. 'As I'm longer I'll have to sleep on the inside – I could never stretch out on the edge.' (I had taken the precaution of occupying this advantageous position before opening my mouth.)

'You're a fly mucker, MacInnes,' he muttered. 'Tomorrow night I'll be inside and you'll hang over the bloody edge!'

We made an enormous stew from dehydrated meat which Mike Atherley had given us – GDF issue: it was excellent, washed down by a mouthful of tea. Don (in the best position for this task) had put on his jumars and harness and eased down the fixed rope, hanging out at a precarious angle to obtain the water by draining the plastic bag spread over the bromeliad. He made the return trip safely and I fielded him on to the ledge. Mo and Joe retired to their tent, from which issued a continuous stream of banter: 'Move over, Brown; you're crushing my leg.' And 'Why don't you put your elbow on the floor of the tent instead of in my groin?'

I had brought my sleeping bag with me, but Don had only a waterproof bivvy bag. We hung the flysheet above which partially shielded us from a cold moist wind which had accompanied the cloud when it had descended about an hour earlier. Everything was filthy and plastered in mud. When I opened my camera there was even water in the cassette within the camera! We were sleeping on a hummock, which unluckily occupied the middle section of our ledge. Don was to sleep with his head at the far end of the ledge, where he was exposed since the flysheet didn't extend that far; whilst I was to lay my head down in a hole in front of the tent. Mo and Joe chuckled at us.

'Bloody good cave just up the face a bit – you're both mad, staying here,' said Joe laughing. His discontent had vanished, as he watched our gamesmanship.

'Oh, we'll survive,' I muttered, filling the offending hole with boots, pitons, and climbing harnesses. They were so wet that I put a Gaz stove on top of them for a pillow. My head reposed awkwardly upon it for the duration of that miserable night; impressing three grooves on the back of my head – the exact shape of the steel wire supports which normally hold the cooking pot. It was a superb moonlit night; the neighbouring peaks stood out bold and stark, like a relief map. Our bivvy was wet: semi-circles of droplets curtained this breathtaking view as I peered outside cautiously, emptying the piss-tin.

'Hey, Hamish,' called Joe. 'Don't put your piss in the water supply, there's a good lad.'

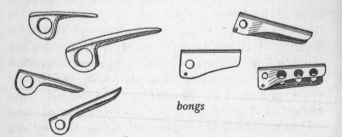

bongs

pegs

Chapter 12

And David put his hand in his bag, and took thence a stone and slang it.

1 Samuel, 17:49

We were up soon after the humming birds. Don was persuaded, reluctantly, to perform an early morning stunt and collected some water. After a brew and some Weetabix, I started up. It had been difficult getting limbered up to start climbing, as there was so little room. The other two couldn't get their wet equipment on until Don and I departed. I swung out on the rope, feeling like a trapeze artist, working my jumars like a rather rusty automaton. I was stiff and sore for the first ten minutes, and, as always after a bivouac, uncoordinated. But it was good to get moving again after that awful cramped night. Soon I felt the circulation beginning to function and found myself in an easy, grassy chimney which allowed me to scramble up for a short way, only using the jumar as a precautionary handhold. Then up that horrible pitch which Mo had led, with the vegetated crown like the arse end of a peacock. I waited on a broad ledge below the strange growth of vegetation through which Joe had led, and hauled in some rope; I was trailing 300 feet of corlene for fixing: Mo had suggested that it would make the descent easier. Below me Don was attaching it as he moved up and presently I moved on again. I gained another ledge, safely past the exotic plants, and saw above me the chimney with a hole at the top. I traversed into it and continued upwards. I met only one scorpion and it was in this chimney, refuged in a relatively dry cave formed by a high roof. Up through the hole like the eye of a needle, dragging the thread of rope, and there I was : at the high point.

The summit was just above me. At first it looked quite easy; then I studied the terrain more carefully and realized that there were still problems. Firstly, there was an overhanging chimney, obviously the key to the upper section as it led to a series of vegetated walls and some magnificent creepy-crawlie ledges, with sprouting vegetation which would have made ideal 'props' for a Dracula movie. I had moved across this large ledge and was studying the overhanging chimney when Don arrived. Its walls tapered towards the top; it wasn't particularly high – about forty feet – but I knew that time was at a premium and it looked hard enough. If we didn't get up the climb that day, I doubted if we ever would. We had overstayed our visit and the expedition expenses were mounting up.

'What's the crack?' demanded Don.

'I've got an idea, old fruit. Just give me the end of the climbing rope.'

He handed me the end of the rope which was lying on the ledge; the boys had been using it for leading. I prised an elongated stone, about a couple of pounds in weight, from the wall and tied the end of the rope securely to it. I tested it for weight. Don looked on with a puzzled frown but, making his usual allowances for my eccentricity, he refrained from comment.

'See that big rock – the loose one – at the top of the crack?'

'Aye.'

'Well, I'm going to try and throw this rock behind it and jumar up the rope when it jams.'

'Aye, it might work, laddie.'

I hurled the rock up with a suitable amount of slack rope in my hand to run it out freely. It arched through the air and fell neatly behind the block, first shot! I was standing at the edge of our ledge, which fell away to a gap, on the other side of which the chimney rose from a lower ledge. I had only to throw the rope vertically about twenty feet, across the width of this gap. Access to the lower ledge was easy: Mo and Joe had been there the previous day and left some climbing gear, ready for work on the chimney. I didn't pull the rope taut from my present stance, but flicked it down until it hung clear to the bottom of the chimney: that would be the direction of ascent and I wanted to ensure that it was pulled tightly into the space behind that big, loose block. I reckoned that there was enough weight in that block to support me, climbing free on jumars. It was a sandstone block, about a foot square and five feet long.

Joe and Mo appeared, like Pirithous and Theseus released from the Underworld. They seemed impressed by my new climbing technique.

'Is this how you get up those Scottish routes, Hamish?' Mo asked curiously.

'Used it once before,' I told him. 'On the first winter traverse of the Cuillin Ridge in Skye. Managed it first throw there, too.'

'I'll belay you from here,' said Don. 'Then, if the stone comes away, at least you'll pendulum over to this side and shouldn't hurt yourself too much.'

'Fine,' I replied, a bit nonplussed by his thoughtfulness. I gathered up some pegs and 'crabs' that were lying beside me. 'I'll away then.' I tugged at the rope from below, then attached a jumar to it and put my full weight on to the etrier: it held. I started up, reaching the ledge in about ten minutes. I organized a fixed rope and then called Don to follow up.

Meanwhile, I had a look at the next section. It didn't seem easy: great spiky plants grew out from the face and it was obvious that valuable time would be consumed, cutting away this undergrowth. When Don came up it was his turn to have a brainwave.

'If you stood on my shoulders, you could probably reach

well up that great bunch of plants. You know, kick foot and handholds – just as if you were back home in the snow . . .'

'Could have a go,' I agreed.

Joe came up and belayed me, whilst Don took up a precarious stance, pressing the top of his head against the wall with his arms outstretched. On his right there was a frightening drop of almost 3,000 feet, into the depths of the Waruma watershed. Though his left foot was firmly planted on a rock, his right one didn't seem to be bearing on anything more substantial than some kind of pineapple plant which was trying to grow over the edge.

'Hey, wait a minute, Hamish,' said Joe. 'I must get a bit of film of this: it's the sort of thing that the Victorian climbers used to do . . . combined tactics.'

I gave him the cine camera and he performed the impossible task of belaying me whilst filming as I stood up on Don's shoulders, feeling like an invalid taking his first faltering steps after a prolonged illness. I dug my fingers into the dense vegetation. I was wearing Don's fingertip-less gloves, but knew that they would afford little protection against a scorpion sting. Then I kicked my feet into the vegetation and, in a few moves, I was up that nasty vertical section and on to rock again.

I found myself upon a ledge, and thankfully put in a peg; then moved up again, taking a direct line for the summit. I managed a few feet, but it was harder than I had expected so I came down and moved right, following a fault line towards a series of steps, about six feet high. They were covered in vegetation and I had the usual difficulty of climbing over the edges. After a while I broke out on to a steepish, wide heathery 'terrace'; on the right a vertical chimney led to the summit whilst, to the left, a series of ledges led up to just below the summit. I felt that the latter offered the best chance, so I moved over left, clambering through the deep and insecure undergrowth. I was now almost directly above the others, having completed a semi-circular pitch, about a hundred vertical feet above.

'I'm belayed,' I shouted down.

'I'm coming up next,' Mo shouted in return.

'Okay, taking in.'

I took the rope in round my waist and looked out to the north. The cloud had materialized again and everything was dripping wet, at saturation point, even under the overhang on my left. Mo joined me, flicking the rope behind him to the left as he ascended so that it would hang in a straight line for the others to ascend to my stance.

'Not far to go now, bach,' I said hopefully. 'I think this line is better than the chimney over there – what do you think?'

Mo looked up:

'Yes, you're probably right, though it's difficult to tell.'

There were flowers growing on the ledge and stalactites of snot – little icicles of algae suspended from the overhangs. It was a weird landscape: straight from the pages of a science fiction novel. Joe came up next, followed by Don.

'I'll lead on if you like, Mo, but we thought that we should leave the last pitch for you. You've led most of the bloody climb anyhow.'

'Yes, I'll have a go,' he volunteered. 'Let's have the gear.'

'It can't be much more than seventy to eighty feet,' I estimated as I handed him a bundle of pegs.

They had a fag each whilst Mo sorted out the pegs he would need. Like some fastidious bird, I picked away the saturated paper from a barley sugar. Joe kept glancing over at the chimney which I had ignored in favour of our present line.

'Doesn't look too bad to me, that finish,' he commented.

'Can't see what the last bit's like,' I pointed out. 'There may just be a through route leading to the plateau, but it's too risky to chance it – I weighed it up carefully.'

'I'm not so sure,' he mused.

Mo started off; firstly, a vertical corner – thirty feet high – and, as usual, thick with vegetation. Again it proved harder than anticipated, but he was given a shoulder by Don to expedite matters. He gained a long ledge above, which rose to the left, and suggested I should join him there so that I could prevent the rope dragging. He proposed to climb straight up from there into a deep vertical chimney. The rope had already formed a dog's leg through the running belays. I climbed up and found another belay under a low overhang – about three feet high. I offered him a shoulder and he surmounted it easily and moved left into the chimney. Thirty feet up, he complained of 'loose crap' and then, without warning, a great mass of vegetation hurtled down. I was leaning into the small overhang, in a kneeling position, when this consolidated lump of soil and plant hit me in the back, completely flattening me. I was totally winded – probably knocked out for an instant. Then I heard Joe's voice from below, calling urgently:

'Hey Hamish, are you all right?'

As Don told us later:

There was a terrific yell when Mo knocked the top of that pinnacle off. Both Joe and I thought that Hamish was badly injured. I thought that it was another Dru job.* The difficulties of getting him off the face ran like quicksilver through my mind. I remember thinking the best thing to do would be to take him right across the summit to Venezuela. I recalled that Adrian had said that the Brazilian authorities knew of our expedition and would give assistance in an emergency, if they had a helicopter . . .

I tried to straighten up and found that my back wasn't broken after all, although extremely painful. I knew I could continue.

'Sorry about that, Hamish – the bloody top just fell off.'

* I had had an accident on the Dru in his company some years back.

'I'll be okay,' I said. 'Carry on up.'

Mo had a desperate struggle during those last few feet but, just as he was battling over the final overhang, his legs dangling in space, the sun came out and bathed the summit in its scorching rays. Mo was exultant:

'It's fantastic,' he shouted. 'Warm and sunny!'

We were still immersed in gloomy dampness. About five minutes later, he yelled:

'Okay, Hamish. Come up.'

I jumared up slowly, feeling as if I had been massaged by a dinosaur. Then, as my head emerged over that final edge, I too was in the sunlight. A broad ledge appeared in front of me and, a few easy feet above, there lay the plateau. Mo came running over to meet me:

'It's incredible,' he gabbled excitedly. 'Like a bloody great aircraft carrier.'

He hauled the bags up, and shortly afterwards Joe and Don joined us on the plateau.

I produced a walkie-talkie and contacted Neil:

'Hello, Neil. Are you reading me?'

'Sure, blue, loud and clear. How are things?'

'We're on the top ... perhaps you would tell Adrian? – "And the sky is clear." '

'Fantastic, chaps. Congratulations! Can you all come to the very edge of the Prow so that Alex can take a shot?'

'Yes, we'll do that in a minute, Neil, and let you know when, we'll set off the red parachute flare.'

We dumped our gear and started to walk across the level plateau. It was a dark, bare table top, variegated by tiny shallow pools and sunken gardens. I felt as if I had awakened from a nightmare: arriving in heaven, after that climb from hell. When Joe came out of the hole, in my mind I saw him emerging from Hades; this fancy was tinged by reality as the sun made our clothes steam, as if we were smouldering. The Prow had been well-named. From the top, also, it resembled the bows of a ship jutting out over a verdant sea. We stood on the brink, sensing a dangerous magnetic attraction in the drop below us.

Painfully, I set a camera to make our own record of this great moment. The parachute rocket soared 1,400 feet above the Prow, then drifted down to the forest. I asked Neil if he could see us.

'Yes, fella, we've got you on film – what a day!'

We hadn't realized then how much interest the expedition had aroused in the world press. For the past few days reports had been printed – some of them, I suspect, sheer speculation – of how many feet we had left to go. Cham had been sending back messages of progress to his superiors; Alex and Gordon told us later that he had predicted that the expedition would reach the summit at 1.42 p.m. precisely on 11 November. He sent this report out the previous day; it was, however, 1.30 p.m. when we reached the top!

Within two minutes of sending that first radio message, Cham was busy on the radio: the code message 'The Sky is Clear' went out to the President and the news was swiftly relayed to the press in Georgetown. One of the local papers ran a headline earlier that day:

Summit day on Roraima
Mountaineering history will almost certainly be made today in the Republic of Guyana. The mountaineers expect to reach the summit of the 92,009 [sic] feet Mount Roraima today. Ten days ago the adventurous climbers encountered serious difficulties when they ran into armies of deadly scorpions and tarantulas while about 330 feet from the summit.

We walked about feeling strangely unrestricted: there were no roots, no jungle, no vertical drops ... just flat rock. We saw a magnificent panorama of mesas: a weird contorted skyline of grotesque sandstone figures towards the Venezuelan part of the summit. We looked along the edge of those fantastic cliffs and saw the waterfalls tumbling down into the Paikwa watershed. About a mile distant was the Diamond Waterfall. There were hidden gardens containing naturally executed statues, fashioned by the omnipotent forces of wind, water and time. There were rocks which resembled igloos. The conglomerate capping the summit was striking: white pebbles stood out in the washed and wind-blown sandstone. The lads were soon prising out souvenirs with their peg hammers. We gazed into shallow pools – like dark mirrors – which, for the first time, reflected man, and watched, fascinated, small black frogs. Mo and Joe explored the north-west side of the Prow, whilst Don and I pushed farther on for a quarter of a mile or so. There was always something new of interest. It was a wonderland like nothing on earth. For me, Roraima is still one of the wonders of the world. What lay in the bottom of some of those deep crevices? In successive ages of erosion the water has cut fantastic channels within channels in the depths of these chasms. There were various levels of chambers; it was like staring down into opera boxes, all delicately carved in arches and scrolls. The point of the Prow is probably the flattest place on the whole summit. The crevices became progressively deeper and more frequent as Don and I moved onwards. To continue, one would have needed ropes and climbing equipment.

It started to rain. We then understood just how devastating it could be. We were exposed to the full fury of the wind and a blinding force of water. In seconds, the decks were awash and previously unsuspected streams started to foam and leap towards the edge of the plateau. We had no forest canopy now, no overhanging rock to protect us where we stood. During the climb, I had draped a section of tarpaulin over myself, like a poncho, but I had abandoned it at the top of the fixed rope. We were soaked to the skin, but it scarcely deterred our wanderings.

'Do you fancy staying the night up here?'

'I would have done, but my back's really sore. I'm scared it may stiffen up and I'll have trouble getting down.'

'I always fancied staying up here,' Don reflected.

We returned to where we had left the others, but there was no sign of them, so we headed back to the top of the fixed rope. Still no sign. We waited there and the rain ceased and the sun came out again. It had lost much of its warmth now for it was after 4 o'clock.

'Wonder where they've gone?'

'Strange,' Don replied. 'I'm not sure if they've taken their gear, or not.'

A bundle of pegs and slings still lay at the top of the fixed rope, and also a bag of food. After a half hour's wait, we decided to go down. We thought they might be exploring some underground summit chamber, but knew that they could find their own way back to the Green Tower.

What had actually happened was that they both felt so tired, after all the exertion of the past few days, that they were incapable of walking far. They had examined the large sunken garden, where we parted company, and then made their way back to the fixed rope and descended.

Normally when one climbs a mountain, or makes a first ascent, there is little memorable about the summit in itself. An isolated point on the earth's surface, where someone may or may not have been before. You go up and you come down. It is rather like opening and closing a door; a fine view is often glimpsed for a short period. The Roraima trip was quite different in this respect. We were in alien country all the time. It was a new and fascinating environment, with the novelty of discovering plants and insects, many hitherto unknown to science. The climbing was as hard as anything we had experienced before; the conditions only comparable to those at high altitude in sheer misery. To arrive on that fairyland summit after such a gruelling passage was enough to make anyone feel light-headed. We had climbed to the security of a huge ship, out of a slimy sea, but now we turned back to the descent.

It was a frightening descent. The majority of the time we abseiled down on single corlene rope, because we had been too short of rope on the last part of the climb to leave it doubled. At the top of some of the pitches it was badly frayed; we knew we were running risks, again. It seemed almost inevitable on this face. As we approached the Green Tower we heard shouts. The other two had come down safely. I felt extremely relieved.

As we were all exhausted, both mentally and physically, we decided to stay there the night, and move down the next morning. We greedily demolished another stew. My back afforded me special 'sick benefits' so I was given the inside of the ledge, though we were all too wet and miserable to sleep. At first light we started to pack up equipment, throwing away most of the things which were not absolutely necessary. I distributed the cine film to be carried down. Don led the way and I followed him. I had promised Mo that I would retrieve as many karabiners as possible on the way. At the site of Camp 8 we met a party of Indians who had come up to carry all the rope down. Finally I had descended the last pitch and, though we had left the fixed rope in place all the way up the face, I removed it from here – the first pitch of the climb – and descended on a doubled rope which I had threaded through a karabiner on the bolt in the Niche. I then pulled the ropes down behind me, leaving the first pitch as it had been when we arrived.

By ten o'clock we were in Camp 7½ with the other members offering their congratulations. We celebrated with glasses of El Dorado rum. Whilst the tarpaulin was being dismantled at 7½, I wrote my last report for the *Observer* which was taken out ahead of us by runner. We all moved down to Camp 6 that day and spent the night there.

I had a talk with Adrian and Mike Atherley. They seemed

unusually interested in the fact that the top of the Prow was flat:

'Flat enough to land a small plane?'

'Yes, I think so,' I answered, knowing full well the significance of this question. 'When you reached the top from Venezuela, Adrian, you didn't get over to the Guyana end, did you?'

'No, not to the north end,' Adrian replied carefully.

'Did you see any sign of troops?' asked Mike.

'No nothing but frogs,' I said. 'It was nice up there.'

The last couple of days at Camp 7½ had been hectic. There were specimens being sent out every day by Indian porters. As soon as Adrian heard that we had reached the summit, the postbags were opened; all that day, and most of the following four days, Adrian was working on the first day covers, helped by Isaac and anyone else available. Adrian was franking, seated at his 'table' (Isaac had hewn a flat section of wood for him). His small band of helpers were packing the envelopes.

We caught up with the gossip which we had missed whilst on the Wall. A 400-lb. tapir had been shot, between Camps 2 and 3, which had introduced a welcome change in the diet. Alex had been suffering badly from a blister on his heel; it had grown steadily worse during the weeks. Cham was hobbling uncomplainingly about on his bad ankle, whilst Adrian looked as if he could do with a very long rest. Even Isaac, who had seemed tireless, appeared drained of energy now ... Living in the rain forest has an insidious effect on the constitution; it stifles and gradually erodes one's source of energy, leaving its victim limp and listless.

Adrian planned to go on ahead to finish his franking at Maiurapai. Next day we all set off behind him. The porters were very heavily laden, but uncomplaining; they also were glad it was all over and that they could return to their villages. We had some Brazilian natives with us: fine, proud

226

men and good workers. They were from Sierre de Sol and had come over for the diamond prospecting but, since the water had been too high for porknocking, they had agreed to work for us instead. We heard that the level of the rivers had dropped during the last few days; our canoes would have difficulty in reaching Camp 1.

I wandered down the root trail with Don. It reminded me of the previous year, when together we had walked down from Everest.

'I enjoy the walk out, Hamish.'

'Aye, no dashing about like a dog shitting razor blades, as Mo would say. A gentle walk like this just finishes the job off nicely.'

Alex was ahead of us, hobbling dismally. He had been on antibiotics for the past week. Both Neil and Gordon were fit though tired. Mike Tamessar, Jonathan, and the other Guyanese had already gone back to Maiurapai to save food. We had enough for two more days. Mike Atherley had dashed off ahead to arrange our evacuation in the GDF Islander from Kamarang.

'Hey, look at that, Don!' I pointed in front of me, at a stilt-rooted tree which had grown up with stilts at least fifteen feet clear of the ground; like the frame of an umbrella, partially open, young stilt roots were growing into the swamp from its base. Don weighed up this oddity and opined that it was a case of getting too big for its roots!

We stayed at Camp 4 that night. Fully clothed, we took advantage of that inviting river and had a wash. Next day we descended to Camp 1 and awaited the canoes. We had heard, by radio, that they would be sent up the following day, but probably wouldn't manage all the way up to Camp 1. We caught up with Isaac and Adrian at this point, but they managed to get away in a small dugout.

Relaxing in our hammocks, we were arguing amicably about bow waves from canoes: whether or not they would be bigger or smaller if the canoes were travelling upstream, rather than downstream, in a three knot current, with the same power output from the outboards. The discussion seemed interminable but was finally brought to a halt by a runner, coming into camp with the news that we must move down the trail to board the canoes. We were now on the section of trail where Ragu had been lost on the approach march. We ran – literally – after the heavily laden porters who actually lost the trail themselves. Only occasional broken twigs indicated the route, but eventually we cut across a loop formed by the river and there, in front of us, were two large canoes. We arived back in Maiurapai at nightfall.

Most of the expedition were together again now. Adrian had asked Phillip the hunter, some weeks ago, to prepare several gallons of cane juice for us. It had fermented nicely and proved to be a popular and potent drink. Two cases of El Dorado rum were broached and some of the Indians were persuaded to sing. Between his cups, Neil waxed lyrical and, before staggering off to the floorless hut, quoted from *Omar Khayyam*:

> 'Dreaming when Dawn's Left Hand was in the Sky,
> I heard a Voice within the Tavern cry,
> "Awake, my little ones, and fill the Cup
> Before Life's Liquor in its Cup be dry . . ." '

Pondering these sentiments, he held his plastic mug up to the light of Adrian's storm lantern and, realizing his cup really was dry, lurched off in an alcoholic haze. Shortly after his erratic, but classical exit, there was a resounding crash as he fell out of his hammock on to a board which spanned the joists below him. Nothing daunted, a few minutes later his steady snore could be heard, rising above the industrious night life sounds of the Maiurapai savannah. Neil's quotation had been more than pertinent. It was already 3 a.m. and Joe was quietly giggling. I saw everything through a mystic haze whilst Mo was chortling as if privately rehearsing his entire repertoire of dirty jokes.

'What time do we get into the canoes?' asked Joe, his efforts to assemble a camp bed as laborious as an aborigine endeavouring to operate an astral compass.

'Four o'clock,' I replied. 'I'm hitting the hay.'

'Don't hit the ground, Mr Hamish,' cautioned Isaac who, with his startling capacity, had done much to help us finish ten gallons of cane juice.

We weren't as fresh as we might have been upon arrival at Kamarang! Mr Nascimento, the Guyanese Minister of State, was to fly out from Georgetown to welcome us. On our way down river, we had called in at Kako village. All the children lined the banks to watch us. Some looked very serious; others smiled broadly. Don remarked drily.

'The ones that are smiling are the ones who backed us!'

There were two planes laid on to evacuate us. Mr Nascimento welcomed us profusely and said that it was indeed a memorable day for his country. Our expedition had created much greater interest than we had ever anticipated. We moved back into the Park Hotel and heard the latest news from the outside world – we hadn't missed much good news. The next few days in Georgetown were very enjoyable: official functions, enormous meals, and long, cool, relaxing drinks in the Park lounge. One evening the entire expedition with the exception of our joint leaders, repaired to a famous establishment, the Cambridge, across the street, where a red lamp glowed above the entrance. There was a dance in full swing and the din was unbelievable. A steel band was creating a cacophony of noise fit to burst our eardrums, but vibrant with that vital rhythm which is only to be found in the Caribbean and South America. The place was packed and the juke box was imprisoned in a heavy steel cage for protection. We were all crammed into a corner when Mike Atherley shouted across to Alex. Alex nodded in response, presuming he had been asked if he would like a beer. In a trice, Mike had returned with a lovely smiling negress!

'No, no,' Alex retreated in alarm, waving his hands. 'I thought it was a beer . . .'

'Hassan again, Neil!' I couldn't resist it . . . "I thank you, O seller of yourself. I buy no tainted meat. I beg you seek another market, and that extremely soon.'

It was time to go, Adrian back to his farm, Don to Patagonia, as leader of an expedition to attempt another mountain, and the rest of us back to our various homes. To each of us Roraima has a strange fascination. The combination of unusual difficulties, plus the torrential rain, on the one hand, and the joy of reaching a unique summit on the other made it an adventure we will all remember for a very long time.

More about Penguins
and Pelicans

Penguinews, which appears every month, contains details of all the new books issued by Penguins as they are published. From time to time it is supplemented by *Penguins in Print*, which is a complete list of all titles available. (There are some five thousand of these.)

A specimen copy of *Penguinews* will be sent to you free on request. For a year's issues (including the complete lists) please send £1 if you live in the British Isles, or elsewhere. Just write to Dept EP, Penguin Books Ltd, Harmondsworth, Middlesex, enclosing a cheque or postal order, and your name will be added to the mailing list.

In the U.S.A.: For a complete list of books available from Penguin in the United States write to Dept CS, Penguin Books Inc., 7110 Ambassador Road, Baltimore, Maryland 21207.

In Canada: For a complete list of books available from Penguin in Canada write to Penguin Books Canada Ltd, 41 Steelcase Road West, Markham, Ontario.